The Lords
of the Valley

LeRoss Apple, cowboy, looking west up the Valley
of the Dry Cimarron.
Photo by C. Kelly Collins, 1995.

The Lords
of the Valley

BY LaVERNE HANNERS

including the complete text of

Our Unsheltered Lives

BY ED LORD

UNIVERSITY OF OKLAHOMA PRESS : *Norman and London*

Also by LaVerne Hanners
Girl on a Pony (Norman, 1994)

Library of Congress Cataloging-in-Publication Data
Hanners, LaVerne.
The Lords of the valley / by LaVerne Hanners.
p.   cm.
Partial Contents: Our unsheltered lives / by Ed Lord.
ISBN 0-8061-2804-6 (alk. paper)
1. Lord, Ed.
2. Kenton Region (Okla.)—History.
3. Kenton Region (Okla.)—Biography.
I. Lord, Ed. Our unsheltered lives.
II. Title.
F704.K46H36   1996   95-36291
976.6'132—dc20
CIP

This book is dedicated
to the cowboys of the Cimarron,
past and present, true lords of the Valley.

Contents

Illustrations

Maps

Maps drawn by C. Kelly Collins.

Acknowledgments

I WOULD LIKE TO THANK ISOBEL LORD, daughter-in-law of Ed Lord, for giving me a copy of Ed Lord's book and suggesting I do something with it. I also thank Jay Ford, grandson of Ed Lord, for providing me with copies of family photographs and valuable information. I want to thank all the cowboys and cowgirls, cattlemen and cattlewomen of the Cimarron who have furnished me with photographs, information, and encouragement. I wish especially to thank LeRoss Apple for permission to use the photograph of him for the cover of *The Lords of the Valley*.

I am ever grateful to three dear friends in Kenton, Opal Kohler and Asa and Fannie Mae Jones. Opal has identified photographs and has told me much about this area. Asa and Fannie Mae have driven Kelly and me in their big old truck to take pictures of this country and to search for homesteads, cemeteries, and old dugouts.

Many thanks to Jeanie Wyant for typing the manuscript and to Roxanne Roberts for typing the inserts. Most of all, I want to thank my son Charles Kelly

Collins, who has moved back to Kenton with me and who makes the maps for my books and develops and prints the photographs. Both Kelly and I wish to thank Ted Mendenhal for his valuable assistance and instruction in the technical aspects of map-making.

Introduction

By LaVerne Hanners

Once I lived in the Valley. We came there long ago, down from the claim on the southern flats of Colorado jolting over the rough road that paralleled the Dry Cimarron River. We came into the Valley through Tollgate Canyon, riding in style in a brand new Model T. The team and wagon driven by Fred Claflin and loaded with all the family's possessions had preceded us by a couple of days. We caught up with it close by the little store and post office of Valley. When Dad stopped to talk to Fred, my two brothers and I were allowed out to have a nickel bottle of pop. It was orange with a distinct, almost painful bite on the tongue.

The store building was on the left side of the road going east back up against the red rocks and piñon trees that foot the Black Mesa. Behind the red rocks, the black and purple slopes of the Black Mesa form the northern boundary of the Cimarron Valley.

Valley post office ceased to function in 1926, just a year after we came down to the Cimarron, but for a

*few years the little store continued to provide a com-
forting oasis on the long trip up the river from
Kenton, Oklahoma, to Folsom, New Mexico, and
Trinidad, Colorado.*

*We were deep in red rock country when we caught
up with our wagon of furniture. The geology of the
Valley of the Dry Cimarron is passing strange. At
first, out of Folsom, the stones, rock ridges, and
outcroppings are all black malpais, frozen lava from
long ago volcanoes. The caprock on the Black Mesa is
a layer of lava from one to two hundred feet thick.
The Black Mesa runs for sixty miles or more east
from Folsom and stalls out just a mile or two inside
the Oklahoma Panhandle. This end of the Mesa is the
highest point in Oklahoma. The malpais outcroppings
continue the length of the Valley, but somewhere just
above Travasser Canyon red sandstone formations
begin to appear. These formations range in color from
the red of dried blood to a soft pink. The red stone has
weathered into shapes of fantasy. Red tables rise out
of the piñon trees, and stone ships appear to plunge
into a dusty ocean. There are towers and spires, a
castle or two, and one silo that I remember. The last
of the red rock resolved itself into two colossal formations only a few hundred yards from each other.
These are known as the Steamboat and the Wedding
Cake, simply because that is what they look like. The
Steamboat towers above the Valley floor, riding high
on waves of red dirt. This enormous butte is composed
of layers of red and white sandstone. The same strata
continue in the round butte of Wedding Cake.*

Steamboat Butte (or Battleship, as it is sometimes called), a
red and white sandstone formation on the Wheeler Ranch
west of Kenton.
Photo by LaVerne Hanners, 1994.

Wedding Cake Butte, a red and white sandstone formation
on the Wheeler Ranch west of Kenton.
Photo by LaVerne Hanners, 1994.

Red sandstone formation in the Cimarron Valley
west of Kenton.
Photo by LaVerne Hanners, 1994.

*These two are the last of the red stone formations.
From this point until the Cimarron flows on out of
the Valley, the formations, buttes, and outcroppings
are white sandstone. The brown and yellow layer of
Dakota sandstone forms the rimrock of the south side
of the Valley. The black lava that sheds from the cap
rock of the Black Mesa mixes in with the other colors
of stones until the Mesa stops.*

*I was only four when we came for the first time
down the Valley of the Dry Cimarron. It seems impossible that my memory of the trip should be so*

White sandstone formation just over the state line in New
Mexico, west of Kenton. Black Mesa in the background.
Photo by LaVerne Hanners, 1994.

*clear. I think it was the color. The flats of Colorado
were endless sweeps of yellow treeless plains, with no
variation in the landscape in any direction.*

*When we came through Tollgate into the Valley I
was enthralled by the immensity of the mesas and
hills, the brilliance of the colors. The cottonwood trees
along the river awed me. The largest plants I had seen
before were the sunflowers by the ditch bank. That
enchanted land imprinted itself upon me, and the
Valley became home. It has remained so for seventy
years even though I have lived in many places.*

*We came at last to the Roberts' Ranch, the first
place we lived in New Mexico. The house was set in
the middle of alfalfa fields and surrounded by huge
silverleaf maple trees. When I saw the house my
world view went through another profound change. I
was born in a half-dugout on the claim and had lived
there all my short life. My metaphor for a dwelling
was a hole in the ground. The house we had come to
was two stories and had four large rooms, a miracle
of space to a child raised in a one-room dugout.*

*My brothers and I began running as soon as we
could get out of the car. We bolted into the house and
up the stairs and over to the windows. For the next
ten years those windows overlooking the yard and
corrals became my position of power over my world.*

*I go back to the Valley as often as the weather and
my infirmities permit. I gather material for books.
One book is already written and published and sits on
my left in the small bookshelf. It is called* Girl on a
Pony *and is about my brothers and sisters and me as
we grew up in the Dry Cimarron Valley.*

*The book here under my hand belongs to another
traveler. Ed Lord came into Kenton, Oklahoma, at the
turn of the century riding horseback from Protection,
Kansas. Ed titled his book* Our Unsheltered Lives. *He
had it typed and bound and then distributed it to his
family and friends. Ed's book sat on shelves or mold-
ered in attics for nearly forty years. His daughter-in-
law, Isobel Lord, gave me a copy with her wishes that
something might be done with it. And so I have. This
book,* The Lords of the Valley, *contains the complete*

Kenton cemetery, with Kenton half hidden among
the trees in the background.
Photo by Laverne Hanners, 1994.

unaltered text of Our Unsheltered Lives *along with
my additions, comments, and annotations.*

*The Lord family moved to Kansas in 1893, and Ed
came on to Kenton a few years after that. Except for
some introductory history, Ed's narration begins in
1893. I write this one hundred years later. It suddenly
seems a terrible responsibility: to establish a continuity in the history of an area, and especially the history of a small town—Kenton, Oklahoma.*

*There is no better place to start than in the little
cemetery on the slope of the mesa west of Kenton.
This place at least remains constant, its continuity
long established. Generations are buried in the
Kenton cemetery. Ed Lord writes of a twenty-wagon
train that came into the area from San Antonio. He*

names families, and those names are carved into the marble and granite headstones in the graveyard. There are the Laytons and the Potters and others who came with those wagons.

The Irish immigrants came. Mary Kelly is there along with her daughters and their children. The Collins plot has a foot-high wall around it, and in that crowded lot are buried the Civil War soldier, David, and his descendants.

The cemetery at Kenton is covered with native grass, and the graves are well kept. The stones at the heads of the graves record the history of the town and of the Cimarron Valley. I haunt that graveyard. The dates, ages, and clusters of headstones record an era that is past. The history of a group of people—the settlers who followed the buffalo hunters and the Indian fighters—is written in the granite stones.

These stone bits of history taken together form patterns. The many small white marble stones show the terrible toll of infant deaths, those stillborn, and those who died of accident or disease. Young children died of childhood diseases that we never hear of now. Ella and Charles Potter lost a teenage son and daughter to an undiagnosed disease. The little Gillespie boy died of scarlet fever. The greatest killer of all was a swift and deadly fever and diarrhea known locally as summer complaint. Infant deaths declined after World War II. Better medicines, vaccines, and better transportation saved the lives of the Valley children.

Better transportation caused most of the deaths of young adults. One or two died of gunshot wounds. A few died of other accidents, but the great majority of persons in their teens and twenties died in automobile accidents. Amazingly, no men were killed in World War II, although one young man buried at Kenton was killed in a ship accident on his way home. His name was Joe Arthur Smithson.

My daughter Sandy and I came from Boise City, Oklahoma, on a Sunday. We were hurrying to get to Kenton, Oklahoma, and then back to Clayton and on to Santa Fe. But first we wanted to go to the Kenton cemetery. Sandy had not been there since her father's funeral.

We walked among the gravestones and looked in silence at the Collins plot. Sandy's grandmother's stone is there and waiting, her birth date carved into it—1896. Sandy's father's stone has not yet been set, but the little plaque is there with his name and birth and death dates on it: Charles W. Collins, 1919–1991. We drove slowly through the cemetery, and I noticed as always the many headstones of those I grew up with, and we stopped as usual at the grave of Felix Goodson—my father, dead since 1936.

As we were about to leave the cemetery, I asked to stop again and got out to look at another grave, that of D. K. Lord. D. K. Lord is buried in an imposing tomb, solid concrete from below the casket to a foot above the ground. Why he wished to be encased in concrete, I do not know, but he did so wish, and it was done. Beside D. K. Lord's grave is the grave of a still-born great-grandchild, and across the cemetery, per-haps a hundred yards away, is the grave of another

Concrete tomb of D. K. Lord (1854–1923). The coffin
is encased in solid concrete from below the casket
to a foot above the ground.
Photo by LaVerne Hanners, 1994.

*Lord child, Ed and Zadia Lord's first born, Leah. The
Lords were important persons in the Valley of the Dry
Cimarron. D. K. and his son Ed were homesteaders,
ranchers, freighters, and finally proprietors of Lord's
Store. The Lords and people like them were the ones
who truly won the West. When the West was finally
tamed, the Lords and other enterprising westerners
ran it. They bought and sold, dickered and traded, and
worked, and worked, and worked.*

After D. K. Lord died, Ed Lord and his wife Zadia ran the store and other properties. In 1938 they sold out and moved to California. Then in 1965 in California, in a place on Seal Beach called Leisure World, Ed Lord did an unprecedented and astounding thing. That eighty-year-old cowpuncher, freighter, entrepreneur, storekeeper, sat down and wrote a book. When I read the book I realized it was a treasure, a true history of what it was like in that rough, untamed corner of the world before Oklahoma and New Mexico became states.

The most remarkable thing about the book is that it was written at all. That an eighty-year-old cowboy would sit down and write a book commemorating his sixty years of marriage is astonishing. That the book is literate and packed with detail is incredible.

In the editing and annotating of this book I have not changed any of Ed's words, nor have I interfered with his paragraphing, punctuation, or spelling. In a few instances I have corrected what were obvious typographical errors, but it seemed to me that not only what Ed wrote but the way he wrote it was historically valuable. I did put Ed's prologue and epilogue into appendices at the end of the book. They contain much factual information about that time, but are now out of date.

I have tried to annotate Ed's book with Ed himself as audience. I imagined what he would have wanted to know, and what he might have wished to include in his own book if he had had the information. In all cases I have set my writing clearly apart from Ed's.

My life and that of Ed Lord overlapped by many
years, but I knew him for only nine. I remembered
him as a powerful presence who owned all the good
things in the store, and who dispensed penny candy
and gum, and who sold me my bridle.

When Sandy and I got to Santa Fe, I picked up my
car and started the drive through Albuquerque and
on down to Los Lunas. As I drove I felt possessed by a
profound sense of urgency. I had just been to a cemetery where I had seen tombstones with birth dates
much later than my own.

In Boise City, Sandy and I had talked with Sandy's
grandmother Marion Collins, ninety-seven, and with
another early resident of Kenton, Wesley Labrier, who
is ninety-six. These two started school together. They
are the only persons left who were born in the Valley
in the nineteenth century. When Marion and Wesley
are gone, the era of the settler will go with them.
Gertrude Cockran still lives, the oldest resident of the
nursing home in Boise City, and is one hundred and
three years old. She came from Meade, Kansas, with
her family. They settled in Kenton early in the century.

(Opposite page, top) Wesley Labrier, 1897–1994. Wesley
was born in No Man's Land. He died shortly after this
photograph was taken.
(Bottom) Marion C. Collins. Born in 1896 in Clayton, New
Mexico, when this picture was taken she was the only child
of the Valley left who was born in the nineteenth century.
Marion Collins died on March 13, 1995.
Photos by LaVerne Hanners, 1994.

There are a few hardy souls left who are in their eighties. The Tucker brothers, Fred and Truman, are retired from active ranching, but they still live on the ranch where they were born, up where the three corners of New Mexico, Colorado, and Oklahoma meet. Ina Kay Labrier still runs cattle on her ranch just below the 101 Hill. Vera Sayre, who was a Simpson, came from the Sayre Ranch up the Carrizozo. She lives in Clayton. Catharine Like Sumpter still lives, but she has been in ill health for several years.

Seventy-nine years ago in 1914 there was a monster flood down the Dry Cimarron. An enterprising photographer grabbed his camera and climbed the mesa just south of Kenton. He took a panoramic view of the Valley up the Cimarron to where it is joined by the Carrizozo. That photograph still hangs in the Kenton Mercantile, in the building that used to be Lord's Store. The photograph shows a wall of water coming down the river. It also shows the little town of Kenton. Vera Sayre was able to identify several buildings that no longer exist, preserving a few more little bits of history. The old hotel run by Colonel Jack Potter burned long ago, but there it stands in that photograph, a two-story building with three windows above and three below. It was a white frame building, and we can deduce that it had approximately twelve rooms. It stood on the north side of Main Street. I never saw it. I wish I could have seen it, but I am happy that at least we have the photograph.

I am sitting in a little trailer I rented from Ina Kay Labrier. I have been up and down the Valley talking *to people and taking photographs. I feel an urgency to hurry and finish the history of this little town. I am almost done. Tomorrow I will go back to the cemetery to check a few more dates, then I will have finished this book as Ed finished his nearly forty years ago.*

Those of us who write about the past always say we wish to preserve the bits of history that we can. We imagine it is important that history have our viewpoints, our unique stories, and of course it is important. But history is not really the reason we write. Ed said it best. "I am just living this all over again." Of course, that is why we do it. Like Ed, I do not remember what I did yesterday, but the trip into the Valley when I was four is diamond clear to me.

Perhaps out of that clarity and the clarity with which Ed remembered his western days has come a book that will afford others a glimpse of a very small piece of frontier history.

The Lords
of the Valley

AUGUST 14, 1964
OUR 60TH ANNIVERSARY

OUR UNSHELTERED LIVES
BY ED LORD

I DEDICATE THIS FAMILY HISTORY
TO MY WIFE, ZADIA,
WHO HAS SHARED THESE LAST SIXTY YEARS WITH ME.
TO HER, I AM FOREVER GRATEFUL.
I WAS NO PRIZE FOR ANY GIRL TO DRAW.
POOR GIRL, NOT ONE IN A HUNDRED COULD
HAVE ENDURED WHAT SHE DID.
BUT, I THINK WHEN I GREW UP
I WAS A GOOD HUSBAND,
AND APPRECIATED MORE AS I GOT OLDER.

ED

CHAPTER ONE

Our Unsheltered Lives

E VERY STORY MUST HAVE a starting point. I shall start this from the time I can remember clearly, about 1889 or 1890. The four children of us, Maude, myself, Fred and a baby sister, Louie. Maude was the oldest, 6 years. To spare details of ages there was about 1½ years between us all.

At this time we all four were left alone with our father, David K. Lord, Jr. He took the four of us to his father's and stepmother's farm house, and left us with them. There was a half sister of his there, also, unmarried. Then our father disappeared. But, he sent money back to them every month from where ever he might be. I think the sister, Selena, was sent extra money for caring for the baby, Louie.

The farm was quite a large one using the standards of those years. He had an uncle of ours in charge of the farm on a share basis during that year he was away. I can remember it being about a year because of the seasons, so very cold a winter and so hot a summer.

Our grandfather's name was the same as our father's, Sr. and Jr. From the very start we four children felt that old man hated us all, and he told his very nice old wife, who loved children, to keep us all out of his sight, so we spent most of that year hiding from that old man whom we hated the sight of. If we got near him, he would glare at us and even spit on us. In those far off days about all men chewed tobacco or smoked a pipe. There were no factory made cigarettes. In the winter when that old man stayed in the house, we three stayed out in the barn with the stock most of the time. Louie, of course, was in the house.

There was lots of work horses, milk cows and their calves which we played with. Also, young colts, and lots of hogs, and many little pigs, ten or twelve to a litter and always one runt among any litter of pigs. These we made special pets of and many, many chickens and turkeys, ducks, and geese. One old gander took special delight in chasing Fred because he couldn't run fast enough, but Maude and I would gather rocks and pelt him until he turned Fred loose. So you might say we all three just about lived with the stock out at the barn all through the year we were there. When it was real cold we had to go in the house and keep out of the way of that old man.

They had one great big old sow who had a large litter of pigs. When she would lay on her side, all the pigs made a rush for the many teats all sows have and nudge each other out of the way to get one. Maude decided that must be pretty good stuff so she got in there and pushed some pigs away and took a teat for herself. She said it tasted good so I got in myself, and it was good! Fred was too little to climb over so he missed out. It's well known that a sow will eat up a child in a few minutes, so we could have been killed and eaten up by that big old sow. Perhaps Fred missed being eaten up alive. I don't know why that sow did not kill us both and eat us. No one in all the world would have cared. That old man probably would have been glad to be rid of us. It's a wonder he hadn't thought of it before and threw us in one at a time, damn his old soul. I hope he went to hell.

That poor wife of his, Hannah was her name. She was a dear good old lady, all of her five children were good people. None were like her husband. He had three children when he married her, one of which was our father, the youngest. The oldest was a girl, Sarah. Then, Bill, the middle one. I am just guessing but I think he was, outside of his father, the king of all the tough guys in the country. I am sure he was with Jessie and Frank James, Cole Younger and many, many other outlaws. He and my father knew all the Daltons. Father was never with these outlaws. He was not a big man like his brother, Bill. He was about my size, 150 pounds. Bill was a 200 pound man and was always in a fight someplace. He had several bullet holes in him. He died at 59, an alcoholic.

Well, after a year our father and mother got together again and come back to the farm, and got us four children home. This farm was about 75 miles west of Kansas City. Father had been a cattle buyer for Ben L. Welch and his two brothers. They were a commission firm at the live stock exchange at the stock yards in Kansas City. So they conceived the idea of sending father down to S. W. Kansas to fence in a large scope of country that had been through many years of drouth. Most all the people that could left the country, leaving their 160 acre homestead claims. So the whole family of us, after father sold the farm, ordered box cars and loaded all the live stock and furniture in, and shipped out to Protection, Kansas in Comanche County.

Just a little something I want to inject here. They [the family] could not decide whether to go to S. W. Kansas or to Wyoming where father spent the time all through the 1870's, hauling Government freight to different forts with oxen. So he took a nickle and said, "I will flip it up. If it is head, we go to Wyoming. Tails we go to S. W. Kansas." The box cars had already been standing loaded for two days, paying demurrage on them. They just couldn't make up their minds. Well, tails came up so he immediately billed the cars to Protection, Kansas. He rode in with the live stock to care for them. The family took the passenger train.

We rented a house in Protection and got all moved. The population in 1893 in Protection was few and far between. The country was still in a drouth. There were actually hungry people around there. Very poor! However, some were better off than others. We went first to the Uncle Pete Wuchter Hotel when we got off the train. They all had the mumps. Then we went to the Aunt Jane Fish's Hotel. We stayed there until we got unloaded, and into the rented house. Aunt Jane had one niece living with her. She was a pretty little thing named Ida and she soon became Maude's very best friend.

The Welch Brothers were anxious to have father get started on fencing in this large pasture so they could get it stocked. Many people needed work, so digging post holes and stringing barb wire was in order. It wasn't long until they had a pasture fenced in about twenty five miles around. During this time the Welch Commission Co. were buying up all the skim milk calves, (some call them bucket calves). They consume all the skim milk as the creameries got the butter and cream. Most farmers just killed these calves, as they were born, to save the milk for the creameries but they saved bull calves as they wanted to run steers. So persons in the business of buying calves sent bull calves into Kansas City to Welch Brothers.

Sheep were being shipped in on account of drouth so these cars were all double decked, and standing ready to load all these calves into. All of them were poor things just able to stand up. They wired father to come up and get them. There were 1000 head and cost from $2 to $4 each. Fred and I, with about a dozen other boys, were there at the stock yards to help with all these calves when father's train came in. He had worked with the weakest of those calves to keep them on their feet and from being trampled on. When they started to unload them, father was calf manure from head to foot. He turned the calves all over to Fred and I and our many helpers and went down to the depot and asked the de-

Dust storm over unknown town in Oklahoma Panhandle,
April 14, 1935.
Photo courtesy of Bonnie Heppard.

pot agent, Will Halseg, to turn the hose on him, clothes
and all and wash all this calf manure off of him. Well, I
will just leave him here to get cleaned up.

> *Ed speaks of sheep being shipped in because of the*
> *"drouth." It was this practice that contributed greatly*
> *to the great Dust Bowl early in the twentieth century.*
> *Where no grass or very little grew, cattle would*
> *starve, but sheep could graze on shorter grass, some-*
> *times pulling the roots up. Their sharp hooves further*
> *damaged the roots of the grama and buffalo grass.*

Broom snakeweed and ring mulley, among others,
were plants requiring less water than the good
grasses. Snakeweed moved into the grazed out pas-
tures and still flourishes in places today. Nothing will
eat it. Ring mulley is not quite as bad, as it can be
grazed, but it is poor quality forage.

There was a creek about a mile from the stock yards
and all of us boys got those calves to water and grass.
They picked up real fast. Most of them were on their
feet in a day or so. There were no fences. All of the
country was open, so we just herded the calves for ten
days around Protection, before taking them on out to
the pasture about five miles east, (Twin Hills). That is
where we moved one of the old houses to that was left
by the settlers. I remember father paying $25 for this
house.

After the calves had gained some strength, branding
and castrating all these little bulls was in order. Imagine the amount of testicles we took from those 1000
calves! Many people don't know how good eating these
things are. All of Protection came with buckets to carry
them home. They were really meat hungry.

It may have been different in Protection, Kansas,
but on the Cimarron the preparing and cooking and,
for that matter, the eating of mountain oysters was
strictly a masculine endeavor. At brandings, the men
sat outside, cleaning and splitting open the testicles
they had removed from the bull calves. As soon as the
women had finished cooking the main meal for the

branding crew, they turned the kitchen over to the
men, who dropped the floured testicles into hot oil. It
took only a few minutes to cook them to a golden
brown. The platter was added to the dinner that was
waiting for the men.

Women were of different opinions about mountain
oysters as a source of food. My mother simply left
the kitchen while they were being cooked, and she
never ate any of them. When Shorty Quimby fried
some mountain oysters at his house, Kathryn
Quimby threw away the skillet.

Shorty and Kathryn's daughter, Reva Rae, told me
those finicky days were gone. She said, "Kathy Rae
[her daughter] and I cleaned those things by the hun-
dred. Kathy is left-handed, so we worked side by side.
When they were cleaned, we cooked them and ate our
share." Then she grinned. "I think I have some in the
freezer. Would you like them for dinner?"

"No," I said, "I don't think so."

We branded these calves "duck bar." The black smith
made these branding irons from a pattern. The mark
was a wattle on the left jaw, so it could be seen in the
winter time when the brands were haired over. This
wattle was made by skinning a place on the jaw about
an inch wide and two inches long so this skin when it
healed over left a round piece of skin a couple of inches
long hanging down. This sounds cruel but marking the
ears were just as bad. We never marked the ears at that
time. Father thought full ears made the steer look better.

We took this herd of calves out to the pasture and

that year it started raining and it rained plenty from then on. Rich buffalo grass grew and grew. This is the strongest range grass there is. It is full of seeds. These calves grew right off and cost nothing to keep. Father's share in these cattle was all that they made less 2% a month interest for the Welches in Kansas City. This was a high interest rate of 24% a year, but all concerned were happy. The wheat farmers all around called father, "the good Lord", as plenty of rain followed season after season and the farmers all got on their feet again.

We had some good saddle horses. We left the farming up to the farmers and we just stayed in the cattle business. We kept those steers three years. I counted them twice a week and Fred rode around the pasture fence twice a week to keep it in good repair. These steers with this abundance of good buffalo grass weighed nearly 1000 pounds when they were sold at $60. There was no loss as the farmers raised plenty of cattle feed to sell cheap to go through the winters. Work was so scarce, father got hired help. They were paid $15 a month and board to feed the cattle through the winters. But the dollars in those days bought a lotta stuff.

One of the great values in Ed Lord's book is his attention to financial details. Of course, he was a merchant as well as a rancher. We see much of Ed's world in terms of salary, interest, and profit and loss. It is as good a way to describe an era as any. If it could be measured, weighed, or priced, Ed wrote about it. Ed wasn't much on lyrical flights of prose, but he knew the worth and the price of the concrete items of his world. A dollar did indeed buy a lot of stuff.

Dad and Mother always took us to Clayton to do our Christmas shopping. There John, Felix, and I were each given a silver dollar and turned loose on the streets. Barbara and Virginia, my younger sisters, were too young to join us, and had to remain with Mother. We shopped hard, up and down the three blocks of Main Street, into Penney's, into the five-and-dime, across the street to Vaughn's, and back and forth comparing and finally deciding. With our one dollar we were expected to buy presents for the entire family, and we did too.

I remember what I bought one Christmas. For my two little sisters I got miniature porcelain dolls with movable arms. They cost ten cents apiece. I bought my two brothers paperbacked books. I suppose they were the old dime novels. Mother and Dad each got a linen handkerchief costing an extravagant twenty-five cents apiece. I'm sure there was no sales tax then, back in 1930, because I would have been outraged if I had had to give up even one cent of my tightly bud-geted money.

When I had my shopping done, I had a whole dime of my own free and clear. I made a beeline for the Nuway Cafe, where I ordered a hamburger for a nickel. These nickel hamburgers were huge, not as big as the dime burgers, but huge anyway. I wolfed down that delicious burger and then bought a Baby Ruth candy bar with my last money. Those candy bars were also enormous, weighing a quarter of a pound.

With my shopping done and my stomach full, I
was able to window-shop. Nothing again will ever
seem so grand as those Main Street stores in the little
town of Clayton just before Christmas. The stores
were decorated with strings of colored electric lights,
tinsel, and large red and green bells made from paper.

I wandered happily through the stores. My shopping was over and I could look at all the wonderful
things that were far beyond my reach. Then I saw the
little cedar chest. I had not imagined that there could
be such a marvel as that little polished, brass-bound
cedar chest with its own lock and key. I went into
immediate fantasy. If I had a little cedar chest like
that I could lock away all my letters, and my jewelry,
not that I ever got any letters, or owned any jewelry. I
was so deep in my fantasy that I stood looking at that
little chest until Mother came for me. I grabbed her
by the hand and pulled her closer to show her the
chest. I never once thought that I could ever own it,
because I had seen the price tag and the chest cost a
whole dollar. I assumed, I think, that Mother and Dad
were on the same budget as I, and it would never
have occurred to me that they would squander all
their money on just one child, when they had five.

Mother took me along to the car. I talked about
that little cedar chest all the way home, and for the
next several days. I had never coveted anything so
much in my life, nor have I ever wanted anything so
much again.

Of course, the little chest was under the tree on
Christmas morning. I was absolutely thunderstruck.

*It still touches me to remember that there were two
cedar chests under the tree. My oldest brother, John,
had bought a tiny little chest for me, the best he could
afford with his Christmas dollar. I kept both those
cedar chests for many, many years, along with photographs of the half-dugout where I was born, and
other pictures Mother had given me. They were all
lost. In some move or the other, the box containing
the photographs and the two chests disappeared.*

After selling the steers father spent the summers in
the then Indian territory south, and across Red River
down into Texas buying yearling steers for fall delivery, on his own time. He would usually buy seven or
eight hundred head. Then in the fall he would have his
brother Sam bring the chuck wagon pulled by four
horses and I would follow up with the saddle horses.
The first year only I got to go. The second year Fred
went, and from then on we both went. As the herds got
larger we had to bring more horses. Cowboys were to
be had everywhere for $25 a month. That was the pre-
vailing wage for cowpokes. All the steers we could not
pasture on the ranch were shipped into Kansas City.

We had no time to go to school. Many families
thought if they fed and clothed their kids good, that
was enough. My last time in school was when I was 11
years old.

Well, back to these cattle. We trailed them from below the Red River in Texas, on across the Indian territory to Kansas. This was not called Oklahoma for many
years later. In fact it was not a state until about 1907.

Fred and I made one hand together, especially on night guard so our Dad gave us $12.50 apiece each month on these cattle drives.

To tell the truth, we were the best hands he had. Especially when we could come to a settlement or little trading post for the Indians. All the punchers would go in to see the Red Lite girls, and get drunk. All that would be left would be Uncle Sam, who was also the cook, and father, Fred, and I. So we four had to night guard until the cowpokes came back. These girls were a real cheap sort. Some of them were Indian girls. These boys who went to visit them usually ended up with something that interfered with their riding the bucking horses. Even broken horses will usually buck first thing in the morning so Fred and I made them pay us 50¢ apiece to ride them until we had the horses broken again. The men finally got well again or as well as some of them would ever get. The "old Ral", as it was called, sent some of them to the Hot Springs in Arkansas to get boiled out, then they would come back and marry some nice girl and have a family of sickly kids. Too bad, but that's the way it has been for thousands of years.

That kind of fatalism was current late in the nineteenth century. Ed at least gave a thought to the condition of women. Most men did not. Women went into marriages without any knowledge of the possibility of disease or indeed any idea of sexual intercourse or contraception. Mothers told their daughters nothing. Perhaps older women felt their daughters would never marry if they knew about the joyless bed, the hard work, and the ceaseless childbearing. Only the situation endured by older single women was worse than many marriages. The spinster faced a life of servitude which made marriage and a husband infinitely preferable.

The unmarried daughter of the house was expected to nurse her ailing parents, make a hand on the farm, drudge in the kitchen, and take care of nieces and nephews. She had no job, no income, and no status. Unmarried women were given the title of Old Maid, as in Old Maid Jones or Brown, and were ever figures of fun. No wonder "girlie houses," as Ed calls them, flourished in the West. They could have seemed havens from the servitude of spinsterhood.

June Davis told me about Aunt Stel from Nash, Texas. She cared for her parents until they died, then became a chattel of the rest of the family. They passed her around from place to place, wherever the work load was heaviest. She cooked for the harvest hands, tended the sick, and cared for the children.

I asked June, "How much did they pay her?"

"Oh," June said, "they didn't pay her. They just gave her stuff. When Aunt Stel died, her trunk was full of brand new dresses and other clothes people had given her. She had never worn any of them."

Of course, they didn't pay her. If she had had any money, she might have squirreled enough away to escape. Of course, she didn't wear the clothes. She had no choice in their selection. Aunt Stel was born in the late nineteenth century and lived and died in Nash,

Texas. The West had many Aunt Stels, more's the shame.

The women who had their own money and bank accounts were rare. Of course, not many women had incomes, and those who did lived in a society where financial matters were completely dominated by men. I remember once the bank in Trinidad called Mother to tell her that my dad had overdrawn his account. The man then said, "We withdrew enough money from your account to pay the overdraft. We were sure you wouldn't mind."

Mother was furious, but she was also helpless. Dad, on the other hand, had discovered a new source of income. To do Dad justice, he didn't tap that source very often, and maybe only accidentally, but Mother was never reconciled to someone's having access to her money. She had been a single working woman for too long.

Kathryn Quimby also had her own income. Her daughter, Reva Rae, gave me an old promissory note showing that Kathryn Quimby had purchased a car described as "Runabout Lock, spare tire," for $469.00. The note unfortunately did not give the make of the car, but more than likely it was a Model T. Mrs. Quimby bought the car March 7, 1927, in Boise City, Oklahoma. Her occupation is listed as "teacher," and shows her salary as one hundred dollars a month.

CHAPTER TWO

Ed on the Move

BACK TO THE HERD. Fred and I usually worked in behind, pushing up the drags. That is the dustiest place in the drive to be. There is usually one man at each side to point the herd, then two or four depending on the size of the herd to work on the sides in between the leaders and the drags. The chuck wagon and the remuda would be way ahead selecting a noon site or night camp, where there was water, wood and grass. The remuda is the extra horses. There are usually six horses to each rider. The horse wrangler is the cook's helper at meal times. Our wrangler was an Indian boy. He was real handy to father for a pow-wow with the many Indian police who seemed to pop up on us all through their territory. They wanted wo-haws, as they called the cattle, for passing through their country. It usually cost us a steer and some tobacco. We had to give them something or they would run off all the horses. This Indian wrangler could understand their language. I had my dog Rover along and they would try to steal him, as dog meat is liked by most Indians in preferrance to any other meat, if he's nice and fat.

We usually went up the old Chisholm Trail, as it went where the best watering places were. Jessie Chisholm was himself one-half Indian. In crossing rivers, some of them were really tough, if the water was high from recent rains. The south Canadian is wide and quick-sand all the way across. We would get the cattle together for crossing. First the chuck wagon would go. It had to move real fast. Then the horses would cross right behind with me and the Indian. Then the cattle would start. Cattle will follow horses anywhere. This quicksand would shake for 100 feet on each side, so if an animal stopped he would sink out of sight in a few minutes. This crossing a herd had to be done just right or the whole herd could pile on top of each other and be lost. Everybody had to be alert and know exactly what he was doing or everything would go down. If a steer got as much as a foot deep in this stuff, we would just as well ride off and leave him because he was a goner. This Canadian was dreaded by all drovers.

The Red River, which was the boundry between Texas and the Indian territory, was tough too, as the water is deep and swift. But if a herd gets to milling in mid stream, those in the middle will drown. In order to break up a mill once, father had to go out there and shoot several steers in the nose to get them turned out and going straight again. A tree or a log floating down river is about the worst thing that could stampede a herd. If a horse gets entangled, about the best thing to do is to get off and grab his tail, as he usually will make it across. It usually took a month or six weeks to get a herd across the Indian territory after crossing the Red River.

Once while we were camped on the south side of the Canadian, it had been raining for several days and we were all drying out our bedding. An Indian and his squaw drove by in a light wagon. In the back of the wagon sat an old Indian woman. They were going to the Government supply depot to get their month's Government rations. I had been wanting one of those pretty blue wool blankets. I had seen the squaws wearing them around their shoulders. Well, I asked the Indian if he would have any blankets he wanted to sell. He said he would trade one for a dollar and a plug of tobacco. He reached back and took the blanket off of the old woman in the back and she was bare except for an undergarment. I gave him the dollar and plug and just threw the blanket over the bed. Father made a mad rush for that blanket and threw it clear away from the bed. I thought he was crazy. There could be nothing wrong with the blanket. He said that all of the Indians were covered with gray backs, (lice) and he certainly didn't want any in the bed.

We trailed cattle up through the Indian territory until the owners of the Homestead Claims began coming back to Comanche County. The drouth had been over and farmers again were having good crops. One by one they came, each fencing off his 160 acres, until our range we had been using so long for nothing was cut up by the returning owners. We could find no fault with this, as it was their land. Father bought the 160 acres we had moved the old house to. Then, he left for Kansas City and again became cattle buyer for Welch Brothers at the stock yards.

Ed Lord was only sixteen when he began his odyssey into unknown territory. If there had been schools for Ed, he would likely have been a sophomore or junior in high school.

On his first trip he was with a man older than he was, but sixteen still seems pitifully young to be so far away from home, broke and hungry. Necessity forced the children of that time to leave off their childhood and go out into a risky world to live in a way that would be unthinkable in 1993. I think of one cowboy and my two brothers, John and Felix, fifteen and thirteen, trailing a herd of cattle forty miles south of Clayton. I can hardly believe that my thirteen-year-old brother brought the six horses back by himself, taking three days for the journey.

Another boy and I wanted to go west. We caught a ride up to Kinsley, Kansas and asked the depot agent how far west we could go on $30 each. He figured, (a real patient man), and finally he had a spot picked out for us. We could go to Durango, Colorado and still have $1 apiece left. So we climbed aboard and arrived at Durango one night, both mighty tired and hungry. I asked my partner if he would rather eat or go to bed. He said, "I'm so hungry I could eat my shoes", so we ate. We had already spent about 25¢ each on the train for eats, so we found a place where we got good eating for 25¢ apiece. This left us each with 50¢. We hunted for a rooming house and got a bed for 50¢. There were already two more beds in there, each had 2 drunk Mexicans in them. After sitting up on the train all night, a

pack of wild cats would have bothered us less so we went
to sleep, or tried to. The bed bugs in that bed were big
and hungry. If we had been as drunk as those Mexicans
we could have slept better. Anyhow, morning finally
came. We were hungry again. My friend said we fed
the bed bugs all night so why not climb out of the window and feed us a little. As it's tit for tat, we'd owe him
nothing, we kept our 50¢.

We went down to the main store. It belonged to a
man named Graden. He also owned a saw mill over near
Bayfield. I think it was around 25 miles out of Durango.
The snow was deep in that high altitude and we had no
overcoats. Mr. Graden was a real nice old man and I'll
bet as a boy he had a bad time too. He said he had a
wagon loading with supplies for his commissary out at
the saw mill. He told us if we helped the driver load up
and unload we could go with him, and he would send
orders out to give us both a job. We got to the mill after
dark. It was cold, real cold, with deep snow all around.
We were dead tired, because we walked all the way to
keep ourselves warm. There was an extra long house at
the mill with bunks all around, built on purpose for
people like us who roved around. Also a place to eat. I
think that bedding had been used for years and never
washed. But it was free of bed bugs and lice. Every Sunday we would wash out a couple of blankets until all of
it was washed up.

We both got up early to get on a job. My partner,
who was four years older than me, got a job first thing,
but the boss said I was too young and that kids got hurt
around there. I told him I wasn't no kid and that I was

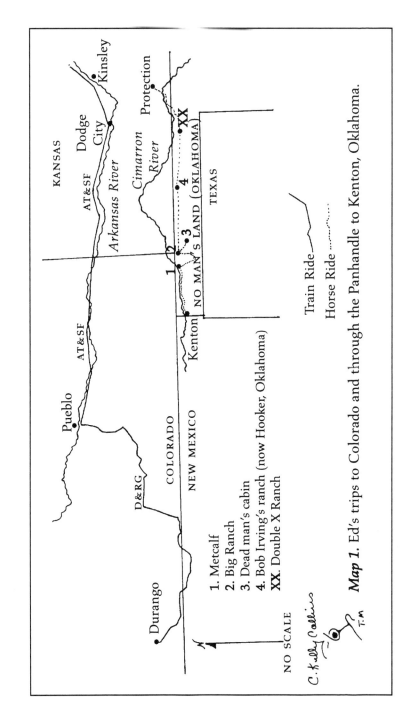

KANSAS

Kinsley

Dodge City

AT&SF

Arkansas River

Cimarron River

Protection

XX

NO MAN'S LAND (OKLAHOMA)

4

3

1 2

TEXAS

Pueblo

AT&SF

COLORADO

D&RG

NEW MEXICO

Durango

Kenton

NO MAN'S LAND

1. Metcalf
2. Big Ranch
3. Dead man's cabin
4. Bob Irving's ranch (now Hooker, Oklahoma)
XX. Double X Ranch

Train Ride
Horse Ride

N

NO SCALE

C. Kelly Collier

Map 1. Ed's trips to Colorado and through the Panhandle to Kenton, Oklahoma.

20 years old. I was really only 16. My friend told him that I was 20, but I ain't been eatin regular, is why I wasn't very big. He said I could work but I should be careful, because the ground is froze way down and they couldn't dig a hole for me if I got killed.

I went to work right under the saws, scooping saw dust and carrying the bark edge to a saw. I cut these up in lath lengths. The ends that were left over I threw in the saw dust box. This box had handles on both ends long enough to walk between. When it was full I would go ask a big 200 pound Mexican to get at the other end and we both would carry it over to the elevator which was an endless thing going round and round. At the end it would dump into a fire that burned all the time to take care of all the board ends left from the lath saw and the saw dust. The Mexican told me that I better get another job, because when them saws hit a loose knot in a board, they come at you like a rifle bullet and could knock a hole in your head. The Mexican told me there had been a dozen men killed there by these bullet like knots. I didn't have to wait for a knot to hit me. I had to let the scoop handle end fall over into the belt that turned these saws and it flipped it round like a buzz saw and hit me in the back of the head and I couldn't remember anything more until I felt the commisary man sewing up my head. He had to shave off some hair, but I had worked nearly all winter and never got hit by a loose knot and got a hole in my head.

By this time we had quite a lot of jack, and no place at all out there to spend any. I told my friend I was tired of dodging flying knots, and I wanted to get back to the only kind of work I knew. Cattle. I decided I was going to go back to Protection, get my horse, saddle, dog Rover, and my gun and ride up the Cimarron River clear to the end of it, just to see where it went.

If Ed was coming directly to Clayton, New Mexico, from Durango, Colorado, he had every reason to wonder about the source of the Cimarron River. New Mexico has two Cimarron Rivers. One heads in the mountains above the town of Cimarron and flows into the Canadian at Taylor Springs. The other begins above Folsom, flows down the Cimarron Valley in New Mexico, into Oklahoma a little north of Kenton, on north into Colorado and Kansas, then goes back down into Oklahoma and joins the Arkansas at Tulsa.

The train Ed was on could possibly have crossed both Cimarron Rivers, as at that time there were numerous railroads into the mountains of New Mexico, three lines running into the town of Cimarron itself. A new Rand McNally Atlas names the river that flows through the town of Cimarron, "Cimarron Creek." The one which heads above Folsom is named simply "Cimarron." I have maps from 1930 and 1972 where both rivers are called by the same name. I suppose Rand McNally decided at some point to differentiate between the two streams. In the Valley we called our river the Dry Cimarron.

There are no waters quite so troubled as the meager streams and arroyos in northeastern New Mexico and the western end of the panhandle of Oklahoma. One of the problems is with the names of the rivers and creeks.

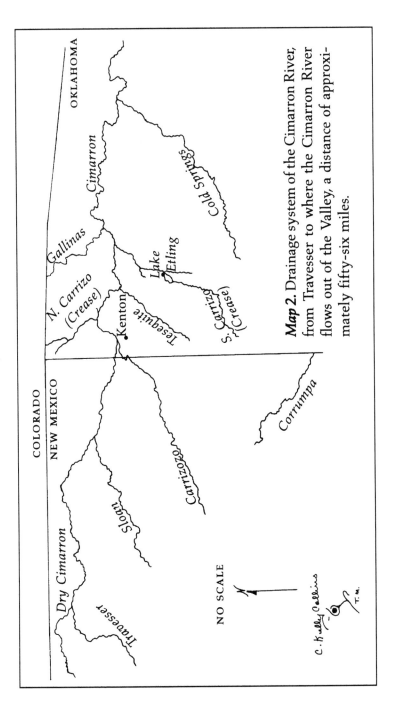

Map 2. Drainage system of the Cimarron River, from Travesser to where the Cimarron River flows out of the Valley, a distance of approximately fifty-six miles.

There are three Carrizos, two Cimarrons, several
Carrizozos, not to mention a Corrumpa that appears
and disappears from map to map and time to time.

The north Carrizo flows out of the Colorado
breaks and joins the Dry Cimarron north of Kenton.
The South Carrizo heads in the foothills south of
Clayton and joins the Canadian above Dalhart, Texas.
There is also a South Carrizo in the panhandle of
Oklahoma, south and east of Kenton. Carrizo is a
Spanish name meaning common reed grass.

When I began studying maps in the research for
this book, I became confused. I had modern maps, but
I had sent my 1930s maps to my son, who is doing
the cartography for this book. I called him.

"Son, I'm going crazy. I have lost the Crease River,
the Corrumpa, and the Carrizozo. I can't find them
on any map." I was especially upset at having lost the
Corrumpa. I knew I had crossed it many times, but I
could not find it anywhere on the map.

"Mama," Kelly said, "just hold on. Let me get my
maps." I think Kelly files his maps by date, the more
modern ones on top. I could hear him pulling down
maps, then silence. "Mama, I can't find the Corrumpa
either, but here is the Carrizozo, joining the Cimarron
just west of Kenton. There doesn't seem to be a Crease
River. Could that possibly be the Carrizo?"

I tested my Spanish pronunciation. "Cah-ree-zo, of
course. That's the river which joins the Cimarron east
of Kenton. It flows by the Tucker Ranch." Carrizo has
been anglicized to Crease.

In a 1968 article in the Boise City News, Ike
Osteen says, "These two streams join at this point.

*Woe be unto the unwary person or animal caught at
flood time in the swift current of the "Crease" (local
term for the Carrizo) or the murky quicksands of the
treacherous Cimarron"* (Boise City News, *Historical
Edition, 1968*).

Kelly continued to rustle his maps. Finally he said,
"Okay, Mama, here's the history. What we know as
the Corrumpa heads up by Des Moines and flows east
just below Moses. We crossed it every time we went to
Clayton. Now it is on the maps as the North Canadian. It used to be called McNee's Creek, and before
that it was called Louse Creek. I wonder why." I can't
imagine why anyone would call a beautiful little
creek by such an inelegant name, but early writers
(Gregg, 1844, and Inman, 1898) mention Louse
Creek.

The Corrumpa was next called McNee's Creek
after an unlucky scout who was traveling ahead of a
wagon train on the Santa Fe Trail. McNee and his
comrade, Monroe, camped by the crossing. McNee
was killed by Indians there and was buried on the site
by members of the wagon train. Monroe was mor-
tally wounded and was taken by a wagon back toward Willowbar. He died on the way and was buried
at Willowbar.

Corrumpa is an Indian name meaning wild or
isolated. A small settlement was located on the head-
waters of the Corrumpa, and there was a Corrumpa
post office from 1905 to 1919. I think it's a shame
that the resounding name of Corrumpa has been
erased from the maps. It seems especially sad that the
grand old Indian name has been replaced by a name

Tommy Hughes—another one-gun cowboy of the
Cimarron. He has his holster rigged for a cross draw.
Photo courtesy of Rebecca Walker.

so out of place as Canadian. I do not know why that
northern name showed up in the Southwest.

I have at last discovered a map of New Mexico
that labels the rivers (to me) correctly. There is the
Corrumpa, just below Moses, where I always thought
it was. The only thing, they didn't put in Moses. Of
course, Moses hasn't been there for years. The map is
copyrighted 1993 and was published by GTR Mapping.

My gun was a 38 caliber Smith and Wesson revolver.
This is a small gun but a good one, and I carried it in a
holster under my left arm. Never in sight like they used
to carry their larger and heavier Colts. By leaving a shirt
button open I could get to it quick enough. I never be-

lieved in displaying any artillery. Most of those guys were a big bluff. I have never in every day life seen a man carry two guns.

So, as I said, I started back to Protection. I got down as far as Clayton in New Mexico, and run into an old horse trader. He had his horses out behind Pierces' livery barn in another corral. He was going east to trade horses. I jumped him for a job as I was going east too. I had no saddle so he told me he would get me one. I knew how, without asking. Just before we would leave he would just unsaddle someone's horse. He was trading horses in Clayton, but the whole time he was waiting for a hanging to take place.

He wanted to see it. I slept with him in Pierces' livery stable bunk house. They had a cook stove in there too so I was his cook. He got drunk every day. He said he had to be drunk before he could do any good trading. Kinda "whetted up his thinkin'", he said. This hangin' of Black Jack Ketchum was sometime in April 1901, I think. I wanted to see the hangin', too. They had a high board fence around the gallows. I walked all around the fence but couldn't find a place to see in. I came to a Mexican boy lookin' through a knot hole about an inch and a half across, square in front of Black Jack's noose. I offered this kid 50¢ for his peek hole. "No," he said, "uno peso." I gave him a silver dollar. They asked Black Jack if he had anything to say before they sprung the trap. He had already told them he wanted a ten foot drop, and they built it so he could have it. Somehow you had to give him credit for having a lot of nerve. They told him he could have anything he wanted for

Black Jack Ketchum
on gallows.
*Photo courtesy of
Center for Southwest
Research, General
Library, University of
New Mexico (Neg. No.
000-079-0008).*

Black Jack Ketchum
prepared for hang-
ing.
*Photo courtesy of
Center for Southwest
Research, General
Library, University of
New Mexico (Neg. No.
000-079-0009).*

Remains of Black Jack Ketchum.
*Photo courtesy of Center for Southwest Research, General Library,
University of New Mexico (Neg. No. 000-079-0010).*

his last meal and they said he ate like a hog, seemed to
have no worries at all. A priest came to see him the day
before he hung. He told them he had rather have a pretty
woman than a priest. I have been told his request was
granted, and they got the best lookin' one they had up
at the girlie house. (This lady said she was never so tired
in all her life.) When he felt the trap being sprung he
jumped straight up; when he got to the end of the rope,
it jerked his head clear off. He was a big man. That head
rolled toward me (did anyone ever see a chicken's head
wrung off, well the eyes always blink a time or two
afterwards), so did Black Jacks. I was lookin' straight at

him. Dr. Slack sewed it back on again. Black Jack and another outlaw was riding down the road one day and a lone old Mexican was riding a burro way up the road, and they were betting on which side he would fall off on if they shot him, so for this they killed him. This was how cheap a life was to him. (Our son's wife had an Uncle who had a small store near Tucumcari, New Mexico. Black Jack and another outlaw asked if they might stay in his store overnight. They robbed him, then killed him. His name was Levi Herzstein.)

Life was cheap in that part of the West, and it seems no life was cheaper than that of a storekeeper or saloonkeeper. Dan Brogan is buried in the cemetery at Kenton. He ran the saloon by the cliffs on the east side of Road Canyon Creek, probably fairly close to the road that went over the mesas from Clayton down into Kenton. Dan Brogan was shot and killed and his business was robbed. He had no family and the cowboys of the area buried him. Marion said it was a nice big funeral and that it was the older Jim and Jack Wiggins who got the money together to put Dan away. His tombstone reads: "Daniel Brogan Died 1901, In his 65th year."

Now, of course, legend has taken over. Two different persons have told me of the sad end of Dan Brogan. One said, "See, old Dan was bad crippled with arthritis, and he couldn't get out of his chair very well. Two young cowboys got drunk at the saloon and carried Dan and his chair outside to the front porch. The cowboys wanted some target practice, so they

began shooting to see how close they could come to
old Dan without hitting him. One of them got too
close and killed him."

The other old-timer's story was much the same,
only he named names, which I certainly shall not do.
I had never heard the names before, and none of their
descendants live in the Valley, so the two cowboys
might as well pass on out of history.

Ed's mention of the girlie house in Clayton started
me wondering about Kenton and if there were any
bordellos there, or saloons, or gambling dives. I had
never heard of one, but I am, after all, still a new-
comer to the area, having been around a little less
than seventy years. I decided I would have to ask
Marion Collins, who, with the exception of Gertrude
Cockran, is the oldest of the old-timers.

I knew there would be problems, as Marion lives in
a nursing home and is somewhat deaf. Her mind is
still sharp and she has a crystalline memory. I tried to
ask her quietly about girlie houses, houses of ill re-
pute, bordellos, and the like but was met with bewil-
derment and the admonition to speak up. Finally, I
gave up and roared, "Were there any whorehouses in
Kenton?"

Marion looked at me in astonishment. "No. Absolutely not."

I asked her how she knew, and she said, "They
were all good Christian people. They didn't have a
saloon either. They had to move the saloon across the
Carrizozo River into New Mexico." Marion grinned a
slight and knowing grin, then nodded off for her nap.

When she woke up, I said, "Marion, why didn't
they have a saloon in Kenton and why did the men
move it over into New Mexico?"

Marion grinned her little knowing grin again and
said, "The women burned them down. My mother,
Mrs. Potter, Martha Layton, all those older women
just wouldn't have a saloon in Kenton. The one across
the river didn't last long either."

Well, if I don't get started to Protection, Kansas, I'll
never get there. The old horse trader got me a saddle
someplace and we were on our way east. We got a corral most ever night at ranches along the way. Always in
a corner so they couldn't drift back west. It seemed like
this herd was getting bigger and bigger all of the time.
He kept saying he was buying the horses that he kept
bringing in, but I began to think he just got these horses
where ever they were handy, and did no trading at all.
Any how when we got near Protection, I told him I was
taking out at our ranch house so he corralled there and
hired a local boy to go on east with him.

I stayed a day or two and then saddled up Prince and
called Rover and we were again on our way west. We
stayed over night on the Cimarron River, killed a nice
fat rabbit for me and Rover, cooked it over a fire on a
green willow stick, and hobbled Prince so he could graze
but couldn't get far away. I spread out my slicker, layed
my head on the saddle and slept with my clothes on
and Rover snuggled up close. The next morning we were
on our way. For a week or two we stayed at a big ranch.
I think it was the XX Ranch. They had lots of hay to

bale. Their dog and Rover did not get along so I moved on west. My next stop was the Bob Irvin Ranch. This is now called Hooker. It is a town that was started by one ranch house. This ranch was south of the Cimarron River, perhaps thirty miles. It was purely a cattle ranch, no hay. I rode for Mr. Irvin about a month. This was a real nice family.

I was now in no man's land, a strip of country thirty miles wide, 150 miles long to New Mexico, east and west. Texas bordered the south. This was all level flat country. The cattle ranged from the Kansas and Colorado line clear to Texas. The next big ranch was a large one. It was hard to get a rider's job, and haying season was in full swing so I had a hay job again.

All of this no man's land, the prairie country, had roving bands of wild horses all over it. I had stayed all night out on the prairie. I hobbled Prince so he couldn't go far. I had gotten another rabbit but had to roast it over a cow chip fire, which is not as good as a wood fire. There were a lot of cows on this range and they had range bulls. That evening, attracted by my dog, the cattle had me surrounded. I was afraid of those bulls, as they could gore a person to death. I couldn't get to my horse as he was grazing off two or three hundred yards. A bull came right up to me. The cow trails to water had worn down perhaps ½ of a foot, and all I could do was to lay flat on my belly in this cow path and hope he would go away, but Rover was right there as scared as I was. Cattle don't know a dog from a wolf or coyote and I could not get Rover away from me. Well, this wild bull had nothing on his mind but to destroy us. He tried to horn me out of that cow path, and finally he got a horn in under my duckin coat. I could feel it slide up by my back bone. If it had gotten up far enough to come up under the collar band, he would have lifted me out of there, but the horn came out below the collar band and split my coat from there clear to the end. I was so glad when the cattle went off.

Ed describes the many huge windmills "all over this no man's land." I remember seeing the ancient ruins of one just out on top on the way to Clayton. The tower was tall and square, not tapered like those of today.

The wheel was not there when I first saw it, and the tower had begun to lean just a little. Over the years on our trips to Clayton, I watched that tower lean further and further. Each time I was sure that I would never see it again—that the next high wind would surely bring it the rest of the way down. I grew up, went away, and when I at last came back the tower was gone.

Last summer Fred and Reva Rae Brown and I got in Fred's big old truck and lumbered out to the Valley. Just before we went down Reif Hill, I pointed out the windmill, and Fred drove over the cattle guard and around the little rise. There in the grass were the remnants of my windmill. I had watched that wind-mill leaning for thirty years or more, and it had been at least thirty years since it had fallen. Those rotting posts and scattered bolts are probably the last bits and pieces of one of the old mills that watered the

One timber from the old wooden windmill. The weathering on the timber is pronounced, the wood having worn away until the nails extend several inches.
Photo by LaVerne Hanners, 1993.

high prairie at the turn of the century. The plains had no wood, except a few cottonwoods in the draws, and no useful lumber would ever have been allowed to rot. This mill was right on the edge of the wooded mesa tops, so its timbers were not scavenged for fuel.

There had to be windmills on the high prairie before the cattle, and later the settlers, could come in. Cattle must have water within at least two miles. Horses can travel farther. There were not many rivers or creeks on those vast grasslands. The federal government recognized the value of the windmills. An article by Earl Cavis, published in the Boise City News, *Summer 1968 states, "They [CCC Ranch] had a contract with the U.S. Government that whenever they drilled a well and put up a windmill, the government would deed them forty acres of land"* (Boise City News, *Historical Edition, 1968). Forty acres of deeded land with a windmill on it gave the owner control of around nine sections of land, a great bargain.*

There were many large windmills over this no man's land. This ranch like all of the others had a wind mill man to grease these mills. He had a camp house way over toward the Texas line and lived alone. He had a couple of milk cows and chickens. Just led a hermit kind of life. Must not have liked people. Anyway, he had not shown up at the ranch for his groceries for several days. So the ranch boss told me to go down there and see if he had fallen off of one of those high windmills someplace. Now, there was no way for me to find his camp. The boss just pointed out in a southeast direction and expected me to ride to it. It was about thirty miles away. I knew he had to leave some kind of a mark when he drove his buckboard to and from headquarters to his little house where he lived while looking after and oiling all those large windmills. Many of these windmills had wheels twenty feet or more in diameter. Very deep wells required very large windmills. I just followed his wheel tracks all the way. If the tracks were overgrown with grass for a few miles, I would just have to find them again. I finally rode up to his little shack. I knew something was wrong when I saw his milk cows with tight bags. I just turned them into the calve's corral and they were hungry enough to take care of those tight bags, real quick. I still hadn't seen any sign of him, so I opened his door and seen at a glance he was laying in his bunk dead. He had a couple of weeks growth of beard on his face, (perhaps he did not ever shave over a couple of times a month anyhow), and he was all bloated up. His two pet cats were eating him one on each side of his neck. I got a couple of pieces of bailing wire and tied them around their necks and hung them both up in a tree that was growing near the door.

> *Ed's actions in executing the cats seem excessive, but it was one of the beliefs of that country and time that any animal that had eaten human flesh must be destroyed. The thought of having one's body consumed by wild animals was a real horror to westerners. Perhaps it was really the horror of dying alone and lost with no one near to know or cover the body decently with earth and stone. "Oh bury me not on the lone prairie / Where the wild coyotes can howl o'er me." This mournful old cowboy ballad creates a different picture in the minds of westerners. Easterners might think of a lonely but peaceful grave with the yapping of coyotes in the distant hills. The cowboy saw the coyotes fighting over his remains.*

It was night by now and I hadn't eaten all day. At 16 a boy gets good and hungry. These surroundings were not too good for anyone's appetite, but I made some coffee, fried some eggs and bacon and ate anyhow. Lookin' over at that dead man gave me the willies. It was raining and that made it worse. Otherwise I'd have stayed outside. I would have rode on back to the ranch, but it was so dark and cloudy, I would have been lost in thirty minutes. So, I could do nothing but stay there.

There was another bunk in there so I just went to bed with my clothes on except my boots and hat. I couldn't sleep any as that feller looked like he was movin sometimes. Just my imagination, I guess.

I noticed a quart bottle of whiskey about ½ empty, so I took myself a good big shot of it. Boy, was that stuff potent. So, all through the night, I would take another drink. It was all gone by morning, but towards the morning I was able to sleep a little. When I woke up the man was still there but my appetite was gone, so I just fed the stock and turned the calves out with their mothers, so their bags would not cake. I saddled up and rode to the ranch. That man had to be buried quick. He was already swelling when I got there. The boss told me to take a spade and ride back there, dig a hole and bury this man, before he mortified so bad he would be hard to stay close to. I told him I was quitting as of right now and he could get someone else to do it.

So, next morning I saddled up and rode on up the river. I had run into some small bunches of wild horses. The way wild horses do, a stallion whips all the other studs and takes care of a small bunch of mares. He drives them to water and keeps all other stallions whipped off. When another stallion thinks he's good enough to take his place, a fight between two studs is something to see, one or the other is usually killed. It is a vicious fight.

Cattle drives to the railroads usually take to the prairie country going east and I wanted to work with cattle rather than a hay job, on the river. To run into this kind of a job, I had to be where the herds usually came by so I went south in order to see these herds. I hobbled Prince out a mile or two from a wind mill and water tank, as the grass was all eaten up near the water tanks and spread my slicker down, put my head up in the saddle and had a nice fat young prairie dog for supper. They are much like a squirrel to eat.

That night a small bunch of wild horses grazed by and the stud resented Prince. The stud fought him until he broke his hobbles so I was now afoot. Prince followed this wild bunch off. I knew that they would be back here for water as other water was at least five miles away. I carried my saddle and equipment down to the tank and stayed right there until this wild bunch came in to water again. I hoped that Prince would be with them. They did not come in that day, so I had to stay right there for fear they would come in to water at night. I slept right there by the water tank, but all that came in to water were coyotes. Along about noon the next day, I seen them coming in. The stud was driving them. Prince was tagging along behind and keeping well away from that stud as he looked to be well bitten up. I knew I could walk right up to Prince and I sure was glad to see him. I saddled him up and we went hunting. I wanted a nice fat rabbit. They tasted better than prairie dog. However, prairie dogs were good eating too.

I had already made up my mind to capture that stallion. He was about three years old and the most beautiful horse that I had ever seen. I had to have him and planned how best to get him. I knew he would be hard to handle being a stud. He might kill me first but he sure was worth a try. My plan was to stay right there at the water tank and keep them from water for about three days, then let them come in and they would drink so much water they couldn't run hardly at all. They were so gant for water they nearly busted drinking so much, so with Prince all rested and ready just a short fast run and I would rope my stud. He learned real quick not to run on that rope because I would turn him a summerset ever time he came to the end of the rope. He learned right away to respect that rope in less than a day. The only thing I feared was he might get a front leg over that rope. He would have broken my rope if he had done so. He was soon broke to lead nicely.

I went on north to the Cimarron River and came to a ranch house with trees all around a good corral and went up to the house. A man named Wells Metcalf, a bachelor, lived there. I asked him if he needed a hand. He said, "I sure do as I am going to brand some calves and work some cattle." That was right up my alley so I hired out to him. But he said the first thing we had to do was castrate my stud as he would fight his horses too bad. That sure suited me so we hogtied him that very day (and took his social standing away from him). Wells Metcalf was such a nice man. I sure was in great luck to find him and also to have a job that I liked. His house was so well kept and clean. I sure had fell into something nice. I liked this man, he treated me good. Why hadn't I run into him a long time ago? I also appreciated the good bed, as sleeping on the ground was not too good and he had a nice dog too. After their first fight (Rover got it good, first time he had ever been whipped they were the best of friends). He even fought another dog off of Rover.

All animals like me, but lots of people don't. Anyway, his dog would follow me in preference to Wells. We, all four of us (Rover, the two horses and myself), had a wonderful time at this ranch. Mustang soon got over his castration and handled real nice from then on. Be kind to a horse and they will follow you around like a dog. However, he bucked hard the first time I rode him. Wells rode him too. He had a wonderful gait. It was sort of a running walk. Most of these mustangs are inbred to where they haven't got much sense, but this one was a smart horse, trim and quick. He made a good cutting horse. Just ride into a herd and once he spots the cow you want to cut out he takes her right on out without any guidance from the rider at all. He was a good rope horse too. Just leaned right up to the animal you were roping and held the rope tight on the saddle horn by backing up.

Roping an animal by both hind feet was usually the way, but branding calves from a herd you would catch them by roping their heads, pulling them up to the fire where the branding irons are kept hot, then two cowboys hold the calves down. One holds a hind leg and one a front leg and the brander smacks a hot iron on in the proper place. My brand as recorded in New Mexico, Oklahoma and Colorado was "ED", high up on the left shoulder. My father's brand, duck bar, on the left side, was one that could not be easily changed into something else by cattle thieves. Lots of this was done. His was stamp irons made by a blacksmith. Most branding irons were made by just plain bars about four inches long with a three foot handle. A half circle, like in my

brand, the letter D could be partly made by a ½ circle or
J-B-C-G-O-P-Q-R-U- and many other figures.

There are a great many brands that the letter O is in.
This one is a joke and please excuse me. 2∿P The figure in the middle is called a "lazy 2". Now figure it out
for yourself. I knew the man who branded it. Naturally
he was just as full of jokes as his brand implies. People
told funny stories in their days too, don't forget. One
brand was a chic-sale, the little building out by the barn
where Sears & Roebucks old catalogue reposed until the
new one came out. I never seen a roll of toilet paper
until I was 15. No general stores carried this item. What
would they have done with all of the corn cobs, and the
weekly news papers? There were no daily papers then,
except in cities.

   *It is hard to imagine how closely a person was
   identified with his brand. Brands were the mark of
   ownership of course and important enough for that
   alone, but the symbolism went deeper than that. The
   man was, in effect, his brand. Cowboys did not say, "I
   ride for Ed Lord." Rather they would have said, "I
   ride for the ED," pronouncing both letters. When my
   youngest daughter was working at State Archives,
   she ran across her dad's brand, the Rocking 8, 8. The
   registration time had run out on it after Walter died.
   Nell called her sister, Susan, and together they
   bought the brand. It is still one of their proudest possessions, although the only livestock they own are
   four head of cats.*

   There were many famous brands in that area, the

*most famous being the XIT. Several stories are told
about how that brand was invented. Some say that it
stood for Ten in Texas, as the XIT covered at least ten
counties in the Texas Panhandle. The more likely
story is that the brand was adopted because it was
almost impossible to change into another brand, although some enterprising rustlers did manage to turn
it into a somewhat blotched star. The XIT brand could
also be put on with a running iron. Brands composed
of all straight lines were valued for that reason.*

*Another famous brand was the 101. The Hundred
And One ranch was in the eastern end of the
Cimarron Valley, but now the only reminder of this
once immense spread is the name of the hill one as-
cends to come out on top and into the prairie land at
the beginning of the Great Plains: the 101 Hill.*

*Ike Like branded the Three Circle Bar, <u>000</u>, a brand
Mr. Like called Three Cow Chips on a Rail. My dad's
brand was the Triangle Z:* ⟁Z   *Mother branded the
Triangle E:* ⟁Ħ *After Dad died Mother sold the Triangle Z to Carl Schaffer, and she branded her own
brand until she sold out.*

An already made cigarette was unheard of. There was
a little pack of cigarette papers came with ever 5¢ bag of
Duke's mixture, or Sheep Herders delight as some called
Dukes. Now the men who were in the money smoked
Bull Durham. They cost 10¢. They also came with just
enough papers to smoke up a sack of tobacco too. Not
one wasted and they smoked 'em up to where the fire
burnt their lips. Us boys who drew only $25 a month

usually bought Dukes. Positively no girls or women smoked or ever drank a drop of liquor, except those in the red light district. Sometimes one may see an old Gramma smoking an old clay pipe, but I want to follow our lives thru the years as they came and I got off the subject here into another ahead.

※

CHAPTER THREE

Ed Arrives at Kenton

SO TO CONTINUE, I was once more on the road up the Cimarron River. In two more days I would be out of the Indian territory, (it became the state of Oklahoma in 1907), into New Mexico. I had left the Wells Metcalf ranch going on west. It took about two days riding to come to Kenton.

Now this little town [Kenton] plays a large part in our lives in this story, but I will write it as it happened. I want to describe this little town first. There were two general stores, a hotel, (most rooms had two double beds in them to accommadate four, when you paid you paid for one space), a blacksmith shop, barber shop, (the barber also was a shoe repair man), a billiard and pool house, drug store, a variety store and a saloon. Had to have a place to drink and fight in. Every drinking man wants to either be your best friend or have a fight. Yes, there was a livery stable too. All transportation was horses in 1901.

Ed says there was a saloon in Kenton in 1901 and that might have been so, but it probably didn't last

49

*long. From what Marion told me, the women of
Kenton would not tolerate a saloon. The one in
Kenton was burned three times, so that enterprise was
moved up the road a couple of miles just over the
New Mexico line.*

*Bud Henry Davis told me what happened to the
New Mexico saloon. Bud Henry's uncles Bud and Jack
Davis ran the saloon, and their grandmother, Mary
Meagher, paid them a little call. She said, "If that
saloon is not closed tomorrow, tomorrow night it will
be gone."*

*The men realized there was no appeal from that
judgment, so they took boards and nails out and
nailed up the windows and doors. Dan Brogan's saloon never opened up again, so Kenton was effec-
tively dry unless one counted the barrel of hard cider
at Ben Clement's racket store. A cup hung at the side
of the barrel and Mr. Clements charged twenty-five
cents a cup. A racket store, so Bonnie Heppard told
me, is like a five and dime store, a store which sold all
sorts of small things.*

*I have found one other mention of a racket store.
In Mary Laswell's novel, One on the House, a charac-
ter speaks of a racket store: "Tomorrow morning if
God spares I'll find a racket store o' some kind and
get us some plates fit to eat off" (p. 108).*

*There was always plenty of whiskey in Kenton, but
it was in private ownership, having been brought in
by freighters from Clayton or Boise City or Trinidad.
The men of the Valley were adept at finding hiding
places for their booze, as any wife thought it was her*

God-given right to pour out any alcoholic drink, or
burn a saloon.

I sometimes lie awake at night and ponder the
logistics of saloon burning. I play out different scenes
in my head. In my favorite of these imaginings, I see
the older women of Kenton, Grandma Potter, Martha
Layton, Mary Meagher, and perhaps one or two others, rise up after supper and say to their children
something like, "I'm just going to step over to Mary's
or Martha's or Cordelia's to borrow a pattern." I see
these women in single file, clutching their long full
skirts up around their thighs, silently circling the
saloon, pouring little bottles of kerosene on the base
of the building. Then I see them striking their matches
on a hissed signal, setting their fires, and running like
hell back into the sheltering darkness. There they
could stand and watch their menfolk hurtle out the
door of the saloon and attempt to put out the fire.

It was hopeless, of course. Kenton did not have any
fire-fighting equipment then, and if a building caught
on fire it could not be saved. I saw the old Wikoff
home burn. It was still dark and I was cooking breakfast for my husband, Jiggs Collins. I looked at the
clock, and at the same time I saw a tongue of flame
run from the chimney up to the top of the roof of the
old frame house. I screamed for Jiggs and for Bud
Layton and his wife Deloryse who lived in the back
two rooms of the house. The men were dressed in
seconds. Then I heard the church bells begin to toll.
Those bells were the only alarm system Kenton had,
but about all the good it did was to summon people to

help save as many furnishings as they could. The Wikoff house was a large frame house, and in that dry year it simply exploded into flame! It burned in minutes, destroying one of the oldest dwellings in Kenton.

As far as I can determine, the saloon buildings were all frame, or mostly wood anyway. I can find no remnants of any of them, or ruins; I do not even know the locations.

I believe that Marion told me a secret that had been kept for ninety-two years. It was no secret that the saloons burned, but never in my life had I heard mention that it was the women of the community who were the arsonists. I think I surely would have heard if the women's activities had been common knowledge.

Jennie Rose Benton, she who was a Brookhart, has written widely about life in the area around Kenton, and she mentions that the saloon was burned three times. She, however, did not say a word about the causes. Jennie Rose did say that saloon-keeping was an unlucky enterprise, and that's the God's truth. For ninety-two years, both before and after Prohibition, there has never been a saloon in Kenton.

Certainly the women hated the saloons. Saloons were hideaways for the men and a drain on a family's scarce money. The women had spent too many tired nights with husbands who were in a state of amorous impotence to think kindly of any drunken man.

Besides burning saloons, sometimes the women took terrible personal revenge. David Collins was an

Marion Chadderdon Collins (1896–1995) as a
young woman, ca. 1916.
Photo courtesy C. Kelly Collins.

*old Civil War soldier from Tennessee who settled in
Kenton shortly after the war was over. One night he
got falling down drunk, and his buddies came bringing him in. His wife, Arlillian, directed the men to the
bedroom, where they put him on the bed. The men all*

Mrs. Horace Hughes, Mrs. W. M. Eddy, Mrs. Eva Simpson,
Palmer Hughes. A formidable group of women. Taken at
upper Easley Ranch.
Photo collection of Rebecca Walker.

*left in a hurry, and when they were gone, Arlillian
sewed her husband up in a bed sheet. When he was
encased pretty much like a mummy, she took a buggy
whip and beat him nearly to death. It is not known if
this punishment had any effect on David Collins's
drinking.*

*Mary Meagher, my older children's great-grand-
mother, inflicted what was an almost mortal wound
on her third husband, Johnny Meagher. She came
down between his ears with a stove poker and
knocked him unconscious. This must have frightened*

Molly and Albert Easley with Margaret and Miller (twins) and Bill Easley. It is said that when Albert went in to see his wife after the twins were born, he said, "My God, Molly, three babies and not a tooth."
Photo courtesy of Rebecca Walker.

her, for she loaded Johnny in a wagon and took him to Kenton to a doctor. Johnny had a severe concussion, but he recovered. When he got well, he went downstate to an old soldier's home, where he lived for the rest of his life.

A woman I knew, but whose name I shall not mention, assaulted her passed-out husband with a shoe heel.

On a picnic (left to right): Roy Eddy, Sirena Cochran, Bill
Cochran, Carrie Palmer, Ophilia Giles, Eva Thorton, Margaret Cochran, Lizzie Potter, Jack Keyes, Maude Messinger,
Dick Easley, Herb Davies. These names are listed in that
order on the back of the photograph. There seems to be
some discrepancy in the names and persons, but it hardly
matters. Any person who might have recognized any of the
people in the photograph died long ago.
Photo courtesy of Rebecca Walker.

It is worthy of note that in all my talking to the old-timers of the Valley and all my reviewing of my own memory, I can find no hint, legend, or rumor of any wife beating. It seems possible that some wife beating might have gone on, if only in self-defense, but I don't believe it ever happened. I think the men would have been too afraid of sudden and deadly retribution. They would not have had a decent night's sleep for the rest of their lives.

Evidently, it was not acceptable for a man to beat his wife, no matter what the provocation. However, enough frustration could build up that inanimate objects were not safe.

Tooter Davis had a notorious temper, but never was this fact so well demonstrated as when his old car quit on him at the Kenton store. Tooter cranked and cranked, but the car would not start. Finally, Tooter completely lost his short supply of patience. He jerked the crank handle out of the car and attacked the headlights as the other customers in the store watched in amazement. Tooter pulverized the glass on the headlights, then turned to the onlookers and said, "I always knew that damn car would quit on me some day."

When my family came to the Valley in 1925, some twenty years after the Lords arrived, Kenton was thriving. There were a bank, a hotel, two garages, an ice-cream parlor, a post office in Mr. Eddy's Drugs and Sundries, and Lord's Store. There was also a little cafe. The livery stable and the saloon, of course, were gone, and I think the ice-cream parlor did not survive

Kenton ice-cream parlor, now used for storage.
Photo by LaVerne Hanners, 1995.

long. The old false-fronted building is still there,
owned now by Bonnie Heppard.

When I was in Kenton last, in January of 1994, I
met the newest member of the community, Brian
McDaniel, who has set up a custom gunshop in
Kenton. I asked him why he came to Kenton, as I am
always interested in how people get to the Valley. He
said he had been a bush pilot in Alaska and other
places and had flown over the valley many times. "I
fell in love with the Black Mesa," he said.

As I drive into Kenton today from the West and
look at the little semi-deserted village, I find it diffi-

Brian McDaniels sights in the Black Mesa Express, a new
and different rifle he manufactures in Kenton.
Photo by LaVerne Hanners, 1994.

*cult to imagine what it might have looked like in
1900. The old hotel is on the right, owned now by Joe
Bud Layton and used as a private residence. Joe Bud
is the grandson of Zadia Lord's brother. I believe Joe
Bud and his family are the only persons remaining in
Kenton who are descendants of the families who came
from San Antonio, Texas in the twenty wagon train
Ed writes about. There is no school now in Kenton; the
last classes were held there in 1963. A small yellow
school bus picks up the children in Kenton to haul
them the thirty-seven miles to Boise City.*

Kenton still has its old school, built in 1928. It is now the Community Center and home of the Black Mesa Club. The ladies of the club keep it in good repair, conscripting their husbands for roofing, plumbing, and other maintenance. The annual Christmas program is held in this old school house and is the big event of the year in Kenton. More than three hundred persons attended in 1994.

The Kenton school house has been more fortunate than the school house over the line in New Mexico, just seven miles away. The Goodson school was built in 1936 and abandoned in the spring of 1963. The children of the Cimarron in New Mexico ride a bus to Clayton, some of them traveling more than fifty miles to school.

After the children left, no one cared to keep up the building, so the Goodson school house is falling in ruins. Rain coming through a large hole in the roof has rotted away the floor in the hallway, the windows are broken out, and birds fly through the classrooms. Soon, I fear, the timbers will be removed for salvage and the school where my mother taught and my children went to school will be just another set of sad ruins.

Lord's Store is still operating, run by Bonnie and Junior Heppard, but it no longer stocks the coal, grain, hay, and lumber carried by the Lords. The post office and a rest room take up a great deal of space at the back. There is a refrigerated meat display, and the shelves along the wall are filled with cans and bottles. There also is a small kitchen, and Bonnie or Junior will make you a hamburger or pour a cup of coffee.

This photo was taken from approximately the same point
as the following photo of Doc Dunlap. The old bank building has been roofed and is now a church.
Photo by LaVerne Hanners, 1995.

Doc Dunlap in the middle of Main Street, Kenton. The
garage behind him was first a general merchandise store.
Photo collection of LaVerne Hanners.

Ruins of old garage just across from Kenton Mercantile.
Photo by LaVerne Hanners, 1995.

*There are several tables in the store, and there the
people of Kenton still gather to wait for the mail to be
put up, to have a soft drink, and just to visit.*

*Bonnie and Junior made the front windows and a
few shelves into a tiny museum. A mammoth tusk
leans against the wall, and there are a few dinosaur
bones and rocks with dinosaur tracks. There are some
Indian artifacts placed around and a few mementos of
the early store: food containers, bottles, and the like.*

*Directly across from the store are the old ruined
stone walls of a garage and a boarded up frame
building, the old Black place. East of the ruins of the
garage is the bank building. It has been converted
into a church, an organization called The River of
Living Water. A car repair shop has just been built*

Log across old road. No Trespassing sign nailed to the
middle of the log just under the knot.
Photo by LaVerne Hanners, 1994.

*north of the old bank. Perhaps Ed Lord would find
most amazing the Black Mesa Gallery and Gift Shop
on the left at the east end of town. This little gallery
carries very nice art and crafts and does a brisk trade
during the summer when the tourists start coming.
Tourists do come to this western end of the Oklahoma
Panhandle. There is a lake close by, and the magnificent mesas. The Black Mesa ends just north of Kenton,
and there is a state park there at the highest point in
Oklahoma.*

*One can still climb the Black Mesa, or go up on top
of that towering formation on a Jeep trail, but many
places are closed off. North of Kenton, I was saddened
to see that great logs with* No Trespassing *signs nailed
to them have been dragged across roads leading to*

places that were picnic and hiking areas when I was young. Robbers Roost, a notorious outlaw hideout in the 1880s, is now closed; Allen and LaJoyce Griggs, the owners of the land, reluctantly decided they could no longer contend with littering and vandalism.

In August of 1993 I drove down to Kenton again and rented a house trailer from Ina Kay Labrier. This is the only public accommodation in Kenton, but it was wonderful, well-furnished, and neat. Ina Kay had left a little gift in the refrigerator, some tomatoes from her garden. I unpacked, then went to Lord's Store, now known as the Kenton Mercantile, to buy some groceries. The Heppards no longer own the store. Junior died in the spring of 1993, and Bonnie sold the store to Allen and LaJoyce Griggs. Bonnie kept the post office so one still sees her every day.

Allen and LaJoyce bought the old Elzy Tanner place, as well as the store. The Tanner place is north of Kenton on the Carrizo. Allen and LaJoyce have established a vineyard there. It is not yet producing, but they plan to make wine when the grapes are ready.

A winery would be an amazement to the older settlers, mainly because of its legality. The Valley of the Dry Cimarron has a long history of manufacturing spirituous beverages. Prohibition, when it became the law of the land in 1920, opened a vast window of opportunity to the citizens of Kenton and the whole Dry Cimarron Valley. Everyone and his brother became bootleggers. Illegal stills flourished up nearly every canyon where there was running water. This cottage industry was a financial boon to the area for

*almost fourteen years, helping to offset the crippling
effects of the drought and the Great Depression.*

*I talked with Allen Griggs for a long time about
the future of the Valley and the town of Kenton.
There is talk that the entire road to Folsom be made
into a scenic drive. I was dismayed, for I imagined
still more tourists coming into this beautiful valley
and trashing it utterly. Allen said that an official
designation would help. There would be turnouts at
the most important sites, informational plaques and
signs to keep the public in good order, and
prohibitional signs to let people know where firearms
and recreational vehicles are forbidden.*

*People who come to this first rugged country from
the flatlands of Kansas, Oklahoma, Texas, and New
Mexico and places still further east become so be-
mused by the change in scenery that they forget the
wonderful rocks, petrified wood, arrowheads, and
fossils are on private property and should not be
removed. Some people are wholehearted vandals who
come to destroy. The plaster cast of a dinosaur leg
bone stood for decades at the dinosaur pit at the east
end of the Valley, but this summer vandals shot it to
pieces. A delicate rock formation is presently under
attack, and each year more of the stone is chipped
away by rifle fire. It will not last.*

*In the beginning of his book, Ed Lord writes about
families leaving the claims during bad times and
returning when the rains began again. Kenton's bad
time was World War II. After the men came home,
and amazingly all but one returned, they picked up*

their families and moved out of Kenton. They never did come back except, of course, to the slope above the town.

There are several homes still left in Kenton. Opal Kohler lives in the old Ford house just behind the store. The W. T. Hughes house, owned by LeRoss Apple, is still in good condition. There are several more, and more are being built, but one cannot imagine that there will ever be many or that the population will increase much.

Since I wrote this book, the population has increased by two. I finished the manuscript for The Lords of the Valley *in July of 1994 and mailed it from Kenton. I came back in August to take more photos. Opal Kohler asked me to supper. Her grandson Rusty cooked for us, frying up a huge platter of batter-dipped squash. Opal and I laughed and talked, and she asked me why I didn't come back to Kenton to live. I told her I would in a red-hot minute, but there was no place. Then she asked me if I would like to have her place across the block. I said, "Yes, yes, I would." We walked over and looked at the two buildings on the property. The larger house is a comfortable five-room house, and I'm happy living here, but the building that won my heart is the brick building on the south. It was built at the turn of the century, a typical early Kenton building with two large rooms, a gabled roof, and a stone chimney in the middle. A small lean-to has been tacked on the west side, and the bricks have been plastered over and painted. I know, however, that the bricks are there—genuine*

*Kenton bricks, made and fired here somewhere. I wish
I knew where. I have walked and looked and asked
everyone, but no one knows the location of the old
brickyard. They aren't very good bricks; the clay is
too sandy, and they weren't fired at a very high tem-
perature, so they crumble. Bonnie Heppard put one in
the little museum at the store. It is still there to witness that Kenton once had a brickyard. Someday I'll
find out where it was.*

*In November 1994, my son, Kelly Collins, also
moved to Kenton, where he presently resides in the
root cellar. Well, actually, it is a finished dugout with
a cement floor, painted cement walls, and wooden
steps leading down. My mother would have thought
it grand. The half-dugout where I was born had a dirt
floor and steps carved into the dirt wall.*

*Kelly's moving into the root cellar was his prefer-
ence, although there was plenty of room in the larger
house and the south house was empty. Actually, if
Kelly had not decided to move into a hole in the
ground, we would not have been able to witness the
event now known locally as the Great Freezer Pull.
There was an enormous old freezer in the cellar, use-
less and heavy. If Kelly was to use the cellar, he had to
get rid of the freezer. He recruited Asa Jones and
Rusty Kohler, LeRoss Apple wandered by, and two or
three other neighbors arrived. There was enough man
power to pick up the freezer, but not enough clearance
to grab hold of it. Asa took a big log chain and went
around the freezer lengthwise. He put a two-by-
twelve board down and made a sort of ramp up the*

steps. Then he hitched the chain to his pickup. Rusty
put his weight on the end of the freezer and yelled,
"Take it up fast." Asa gunned the pickup and the
freezer erupted from the cellar like a whale coming
up for air, or like a torpedo. Actually it looked like
nothing so much as a large white freezer exploding
out of the ground. I'll never forget that sight.

The freezer provided a door for Kelly's cellar. There
had been a wooden door over the entrance, but it
broke in two in a high wind. Kelly took off the lid to
the freezer and hinged it to the facing around the
door. I feel a little silly sometimes when I pull the
freezer door up and yell down the steps to roust out
my only son. Then again, perhaps he feels a little silly
that the first thing to meet his eyes when he climbs
up out of his cellar is his mother's bottle tree.

I always wanted a bottle tree, but I never had a
chance for one until I moved back to Kenton. There in
the backyard was a small dead tree. I carefully
pruned it, leaving stubs of branches turning upward.
Then I jammed bottles down on the stubs. I still have
stubs left, and just this morning someone tippy-toed
up and hung a lovely green bottle on one of the
empty branches.

That is the sort of thing that typifies this little
town. No one else has a bottle tree nor, I suspect,
would want one. However, if a neighbor wants one,
others are willing to aid and abet.

I seen an old man leaning up against the hitch rack
where all the horses were tied. He was full whiskered

Bottle tree and freezer-lid door, two of the unnatural
wonders of Kenton.
Photo by LaVerne Hanners, 1995.

and gray and seemed to be about 60. I was leaning
there also. He was chewin' tobacco, spitting at a rock.
Seemed to be hitting it ever time. He pulled out his
plug and said, "Wanna chew, kid?" To be friendly I
said, "sure." We got to talking. He said, "Does your
dog know anything about smellin out game?" I said,
"He can find game where there ain't any." "Say", he
said, "you need a job?" I said, "I sure do." He had a
horse hooked to a four wheel buckboard, which is a
vehicle without springs. Just the springs in the boards
the bottom was made of. "Well," he said, "you just tie
your hosses along side and we will go. It's about
twenty miles up to my shack in New Mexico where I
am trapping for furs and what we make is half yours.

I believe that Tex and Ed have their distances wrong. Further descriptions of Tex's shack place it in Sloan Canyon. (Ed calls it "Slone.") The shack must have been built close to the first spring in the canyon, a distance of hardly ten miles. It must have seemed much further on a horse, or in a buggy.

This old man was from way down in Texas and he was just Tex to everybody. I don't suppose anyone ever heard his last name. He could not read or even write his name. We got up there way after night, hobbled all the horses, cooked some supper and went to bed.

He had an old wood bedstead and some awful dirty old blankets. He had a pillow filled with cotton. I used my clothes for a pillow. He had a kerosene lantern. I was sure tired but those bed bugs in that bed were the hungriest bugs I ever slept with. They all came over to my side, he was old and tough so they fed on me all night. I was more tender, I guess. I got thru the night, but there was more bed bugs in that one bed. They must have run over each other to get to me. I asked Tex if I may take the mattress. It was a straw mattress outside and to get the bugs off, I cleaned around the tufts with a feather dipped in kerosene. I shook out all the blankets and aired them in the sun. When I made up the bed again I set each leg in a can with about ¼ inch of kerosene in it, so these bugs couldn't crawl up the legs, pulled it clear of the walls. So the bed bug situation was solved.

I was a good cook, so while he was out riding the trap line I had ever thing cleaned up. I even washed the half window. This shack had a dirt roof and dirt floor so he could spit anywhere, a small fireplace in one corner and one door. It was partly dug in the south side of a hill, so the north wall was partly a dirt wall. A large log across the top center supported a roof with small poles to the walls from this center log. Keep this little dug out in mind because in three years from now it plays an important part in our lives. Well we got along just fine, Tex and I. He had a heart as big as a bucket. We took out many furs the rest of that winter with the exception of the time lost when he got hurt so bad.

> *The shack that Ed describes here, and writes about later on, has proven to be most elusive. Kelly and I, along with Asa and Fannie Mae Jones, have searched the mesas on the east side of Sloan Canyon looking for the site of the shack. It must lie on the east side because Ed's description places it near Sloan Creek. We have not found the little half-dugout yet, and it may be that no trace of it exists. There is a large arroyo in just about the only location that fits Ed's description. Human habitation leaves little ruts and scars on the land that hasten erosion, so it may be that the little shack has washed away.*

In addition to trapping we cut cedar posts to sell. These mesa tops were covered with yellow cedar trees that make the longest lasting fence posts. Some posts of this type of cedar were used by the old 101 Ranch in 1870. They were still in good condition in the ground in 1901. We dragged them on a sled to the mesa cap rock edge. We had a galvanized wire size 9, using two fence staples, one at the top and one at the bottom, tacked these posts on one at a time and they slid clear to the

bottom of the canyon, butt end down on this wire. We
had a knot at the bottom and that would knock these
staples off letting the posts all fall in a pile so wagons
could load them up at 10¢ each. They came from as far
as 40 miles for these posts, as we cut only straight posts.
Well, one day Tex fell off this cap rock about twenty
feet into a cedar tree. Had that tree not been there he
would have fallen into rock and been killed instantly. I
got down to him as fast as I could to get him out of that
tree and down to the buckboard so I could haul him in
to the cabin. His right leg and left arm were broken
below the knee and elbow and he was hurt in his back,
but I dragged him down the mesa side through the boulders and brush. It took me a couple of hours as I rested
him and myself in the shade of boulders clear to the
bottom, then loaded him into the buckboard and took
him to the cabin. These mesas, I should judge to be about
500 feet high on about a 40 degree slant up to the top of
the cap rock. First thing to do was give him some whiskey. He hurt terrible, then put some splints on his leg
and arm before they swelled too bad. He always kept
his wooden boxes he got groceries in, there was no card
board boxes in them days. From these I made splints.
He had no cord except a short clothes line, but he did
have bailing wire. Everbody used to keep all the hay
bale wires. Anything could be fixed with bailing wire. I
felt them bones good so I could join them up as best I
could and strapped them on tight. When he wanted to
turn over in bed I rolled him over. I was so glad he had
that whiskey.

      That poor guy sure hurt. I never left him except to
go to the spring for water about one-fourth mile down

the canyon. I rode over to our nearest neighbor [*Smylie?*] five miles away and told them to bring some groceries. We had no doctor in the country, so it was another quart of whiskey. For two weeks I stayed right by Tex's bedside. He hurt worse than any human I ever saw but I could see he was getting better ever day. I just made him eat good. I was so glad he was getting well. These old Texans are mighty hard to kill and I am sure if it had been me instead of him, he would have taken care of me.

After about a month Tex was once more on his feet. One day I asked him if he ever took a bath. He said no because he never got dirty enough yet to take one, so since I hadn't been swimmin for months, I told him I was going to scrub off some of my scale. "Now Eddie," he said, "that's plumb foolish but iffen you do go to all that trouble don't do it in the water hole where the horses drink, find another water hole, because horses won't drink in water that has had soap in it." So I took a bath, the first one in months and it didn't make me sick like Tex said it would. Water is to drink and for fish, he said.

When I read Ed's account of his yearly bath, I remembered vividly Al Dick, an elderly cowboy on our ranch. He had a head of thick black hair. He told us kids he had no gray in his hair because he never had washed it. Not until I read Ed's story did I believe Old Man Dick. Cowboys really didn't bathe, at least not much.

I called my brother Felix, who had gone to the bunkhouse when he was three, and asked him about

cowboy hygiene. He told me that the cowboys bathed
occasionally, heating a teakettle of water on the heating stove and pouring it into a number two washtub.
Mother retrieved her two boys from the bunkhouse
every Saturday and forced them to bathe and put on
clean underwear. I can't imagine how our small
kitchen must have smelled with three or four un-
washed cowboys, five nasty little kids, and perhaps, in
a box behind the stove, a few baby chickens.

Perhaps cowboys smell a lot better now, what with
all the shampoos, perfumes, and soap that advertisers
are promoting. The image of the cowboy is evidently
a powerful selling agent. The Stetson hat now sells
perfume, and so do the leather leggings cowboys wear
to protect their legs.

The Stetson hat was as much a part of the cowboy
as his pants. He took off his hat in church, or in any
house, or when he was being introduced to or meeting
a woman, but otherwise his hat was on his head.
When a cowboy did take off his hat, his forehead
shone a pearly white. In the picture of the Like family, Joe is wearing his Stetson, but Chester on the left,
and Everett on the right, have removed their hats,
plainly showing their untanned foreheads. I have
always thought that the white forehead above the
weather-beaten brown face was the mark of the true
working cowboy. I still see it in my visits to Clayton
and to Kenton, where there are left a few, a very few,
honest-to-God cowboys.

Stetson hats lasted for years and got heavier and
greasier as time went by. A Stetson was useful for

The Isaac Like family, late 1950s. Back row, Chester, Joe,
Catherine Like Sumpter, and Everett. Front row, Isaac Like,
Mrs. Like, and Wilma Like Sumpter.
Photo courtesy of Jane Like.

*fanning a stubborn campfire into flame; it was good
for carrying water or using as a feed bag for a horse.
This wonderful western hat protected its wearer from
sun, wind, rain, snow, sleet, and hail.*

*About the only beauty aid available to cowboys
was a cheap hair oil, colored red and loudly odorous.
The brand name was Brilliantine, and cowboys used a
lot of it. This oil, mixed with sweat, gradually soaked
through a cowboy's hat, picking up layers of dust.
Stetsons could be cleaned and reblocked, eliminating
some of the rancid oil and dirt, but never, never did a
Stetson hat smell good.*

The leather leggings cowboys wore originated in the Big Bend area of Texas where chaparral grows profusely. This densely growing shrub whipped and stung a rider's legs and caused considerable discomfort. Finally, some tortured but enterprising cowboy cobbled himself a pair of seatless leather pants. This garment proved so useful that soon cowboys everywhere were wearing them. If he was a Mexican cowboy or vaquero *he called his leather pants* chaparreros, *which means, "Those leather pants I wear when I am riding in the chaparral." The Texan called his leather pants* chaps, *which means, "Those leather pants I wear. . . ." The word* chaps *is pronounced* shaps *as in shoot, not* chaps *as we hear almost daily in that perfume advertisement that always makes me shudder. Of course, there is always the faint hope that the manufacturers of the perfume are referring to the British word* chap, *meaning man.*

Like the Stetson, leather chaps did come to symbolize the cowboy. Chaps were the cowboy's own unique article of apparel, but never, never did a pair of chaps smell good.

The older cowboys were not as fashion conscious as the ones in the twenties and thirties whom I knew in my childhood. After all, Ed spent most of his time in the company of Tex, who had never bathed in his life. There wasn't much point in dressing up. I am sure that Ed did provide himself with clean clothes when he was riding out to the dances. I don't know if Ed's wardrobe would have included a white shirt or not, but by the time I was growing up the white shirt was

Three cowboys of the area: Bud Henry Davis, Miller
Easley, and Jimmy Wiggins, ca. 1939.
Photo courtesy of Rebecca Walker, granddaughter of Miller Easley.

Laughing cowboy (Junior Labrier).
Photo by LaVerne Hanners, 1994.

*essential to the dressed-up cowboy. I have a videotape
of cowboys preparing for a rodeo. The sixteen-milli-
meter film from which the tape was made was shot
by Simon Herzstein in the early thirties. The film
shows cowboys on the streets of Clayton getting
ready for a rodeo. They are all wearing white shirts
and looking like members of a boys' choir. They all
have on enormous Stetsons. I told a friend, Miki
Thornburg, about those hats. She said, "Yeah, my
brother bought one of them once. Dad said he looked
like a pissant under a cow chip."*

A group of jolly cowboys, Kenton Mercantile.
Photo by LaVerne Hanners, 1994.

*Although the cowboys of Kenton still wear
Stetsons, and many wear chaps when they are working, the white shirts seem to have given way to
striped ones or ones of dark color. I haven't seen a
cowboy in a white shirt in years, unless maybe with a
suit at a wedding or a funeral.*

*I suspect World War II had something to do with
the demise of the white shirt for the working cowboy.
Most of the cowboys I knew got used to wearing olive
drab or khaki.*

Leon Apple on Gus and LeRoss Apple on Goose in front of
Kenton Mercantile, built in 1904 by D. K. Lord and his sons
Ed and Fred.
Photo by Allen Griggs, 1994.

Tex finally got well. One day he asked me if I knew
another Lord in this country called Duck Lord. I said
no, but I got to thinkin' about this Duck brand of my
fathers, so I thought I would just ride over into this
other canyon and see him. It was my father, sure
enough.

All this New Mexico country except the Cimarron

River and other big water courses was all Government land. All unfenced free range. Father was living in a tent and was sent out in this open free range country by the same Welch Bros. Commission Co. in Kansas City who sent him down in Texas to buy and trail up thru the Indian Territory, cattle to put on the good buffalo grass in Kansas. I previously mentioned this grass was also free. After the settlers moved back to their claims in Kansas, this broke up that situation there and father came west looking for free range again. He had lost most of his money. As I also said before, he was a good gambler. But he was also a hard drinker so he lost most of his money whenever he drank too much. One has to have a clear head to win at cards. But he [D. K. Lord] was a good judge of cattle and a very good buyer, so these Welch Bros. wanted him to buy 1000 yearling steers and take care of them as in Kansas. The difference was the range in Kansas was all prairie land and fenced while this New Mexico deal was free range, unfenced, all rough canyon land. They were just turned loose with thousands of other cattle. General round-up in the fall which all cattle men attended with their own chuck wagon and riders, gathered their own cattle at these round-ups. Each cutting out his own stock and driving them home to their own ranges.

Father had filed on a watered claim in order to have head quarters on an established locality.

Ed says his dad had filed on a "watered claim" and then a few pages further on Ed says that water was far off, and while he was working for his dad they

hauled water from the shack where Ed and Tex had
lived. Two explanations are possible. In New Mexico
springs of water can be seasonal, appearing and dis-
appearing as the weather changes, and there may
have been a spring of drinkable water there when
D. K. Lord filed on the place. On the other hand, a
"watered claim" may have just meant a water hole
for stock, with no water for drinking. A desert claim,
of course, meant that there was no water at all on the
land.

Father said, "Ed, if you want a job you can have one here at $35 a month instead of the usual $25. You will have a more responsible position here than most cow-pokes because I will be away part time." I caught on quick. He wanted to be somewhere playing poker, once he had someone he could trust with his herd of steers. Well, he was too old now to change, so I told him I would batch here and look after the steers. I would go over and see Tex ever two or three days or he would come over and see me. We played cards a lot to pass away the evenings. But I was real busy with these steers as I tried to keep them on the range near our water. When the hair got long in winter and brands were hard to see, they all carried the same wattle on the left jaw as in Kansas so it was easy to spot that mark.

If I needed any help, old Tex was always ready. Fa-ther was home part of the time, and he liked old Tex too. One time I got a tooth ache and it ached night and day. Father and old Tex decided it just had to come out. Pliers were unknown at that time, so Tex went to Kenton one day for supplies for him and us, too. Father told him to have the blacksmith, John Youngblood, make an instrument to pull my tooth out. That was the achinest tooth I or anyone else ever had. He came by our tent and left our supplies and the tooth puller and told us he would be back the next day and would pull that tooth hisself. He, the barber and the blacksmith talked it all over down at Kenton and they concluded they would give me enough whiskey so I wouldn't hurt so bad when he pulled it out. They couldn't decide how much of it to give me so he told father I should sit on a box until I had taken enough that I would fall over then I would be ready. Father always had plenty of it, so I was hurtin' so bad they decided to get it over with. I wish I had kept those forceps, but the tool looked like they could get the job done. So I started on the whiskey and I really didn't know when the job was over. My mouth was good and sore. I was two days getting sober again, but the toothache was gone. The cavity was between two teeth clear to the nerve in the tooth. I kept that tooth just to look at for over forty years.

While my aches and pains are on my mind, I will tell of another incident. I had what I thought was a tick in my ear. Father said tobacco juice would bring it out. He spit tobacco juice in it for three days and it only got worse. Mrs. Smylie, a widow lady who borned all the babies in the country, and if anybody got sick she was the first one people thought of, anyway I rode down there and by that time my tooth ache was mild compared to that pain way down in my ear. I wished somebody would shoot me. I layed on the side of the bed and she kept hot packs on that ear day and night for two days. I know she never slept in all that time. The third day that ear broke loose inside and the pus just squirted out. I had a rising way down in that ear, and it run out for two or three days afterward. That was the winter of 1902-1903. That dear, dear old woman. She has been dead many, many years. I woulda went to hell for that good old woman. I always think I will put up a tombstone for her someday. She lies beside her nice husband, Samuel Smylie who has a tombstone at his grave, way back in Kenton, Oklahoma, where my father lies, also our first child Leah, who was killed in 1905. This story follows later. Also most of Zadia's folks are buried there.

Smylie's ranch was headquartered at Cottonwood Springs, at the mouth of the canyon just east of Sloan Canyon. In 1932 my dad, Felix Goodson, bought the Smylie Ranch and tore down the old Smylie house for the adobes and lumber. They moved this building material three quarters of a mile east and built a new house there. I was in the old Smylie house once before it was destroyed. In my child's memory it was a huge place, with many rooms. The adobes in the walls were eighteen inches square, and there were enough of them for Dad to build a large three-bedroom home. The lumber for the Smylie house had been hauled from Trinidad by wagon, and the house was put together with old wrought-iron nails.

I called Willie Benevidez when I was in Kenton in the summer of 1993. He is foreman of all the Cliff Skiles holdings in the Valley, including our old ranch.

I told him I would like to see the house and the ranch, if possible, and take some photographs. I met him at the headquarters of the Black Mesa Ranch, the place where we lived when we first came to the Valley. The giant silver-leafed maple trees are gone now, but they have planted groves of other trees that are still only saplings.

We went on up to the old Goodson Ranch near the south mesas and drove all around it. Mr. Skiles has done a massive soil reclamation project, throwing vast earth dams across the eroding arroyos. We came back by Cottonwood Springs. There are no trees at the springs now, and finally I realized what was bothering me. I was older than I thought, having outlived the maples, the cottonwoods, and the Chinese elms. These fast-growing trees have a short life-span, comparatively speaking. The maples were planted when the country was settled and lasted less than a century. My mother planted the Chinese elms around the house, and they lived out their allotted span of fifty or sixty years. I was sad to see the beautiful, enormous old trees were gone but glad that the new owner had replaced them with saplings.

We stopped at the ranch house. The interior looked much as it had when we first moved into it in 1935. The outside of the house has been changed completely. The brown adobe of the walls has been stuccoed and painted white, and instead of the old brown shingles there is a gleaming red tile roof. The house is now a hunting lodge. It was strange to see bunks in what was my room.

*We hope to go back there in the summer of 1994.
All of Felix Goodson's descendants—the boys raised
in a college town in Massachusetts, the young men
and women from California, the Texans from San
Antonio, the boys from Detroit, the girls from Virginia, the young people from Indiana, my daughter
and her daughter from Arizona, and my two daughters who still live in New Mexico—want to meet in
the Valley to see the vast empty country they came
from.*

*My mother, Stella Goodson, was a teacher, and
most of her descendants have been brainwashed
about the value of an education. I want her grandchildren and great-grandchildren to see the ruins of
the school where she taught. I look forward to their
standing at the point of the big hill and looking up
the valley to the old Roberts Ranch. I want them to
imagine, if they can, five children—John, LaVerne,
Felix, Virginia, and Barbara—running all the way
from the ranch house to the school and running all
the way back.*

*Sometimes Mrs. Quimby taught at the New
Mexico school and Mother taught at the Wagner*

(Opposite, top:) Ruins of New Mexico schoolhouse. The
room in the back was provided for the teacher to live in.
(Bottom:) New Mexico schoolhouse ruins, showing the
plastered sections of the wall that served as blackboards. Of
course, the black paint washed away many years ago.
Both photos by LaVerne Hanners, 1994.

View of the Valley floor looking east toward Kenton, taken
from the point of the mesa just west of the New Mexico
schoolhouse. Ruins of the schoolhouse are in the lower
right corner.
Photo by Fred Brown, 1992, collection of LaVerne Hanners.

*school, but always the Goodson children and the
Wigginses attended the stone building shown below.
The smooth patches on the rock walls were areas that
were finished with a smooth hard plaster. This plaster
was painted with black paint for blackboards. These
blackboards and white chalk were the only teaching
aids my mother or Kathryn Quimby had. Except,
now that I think back, both teachers used a device
called a hecktograph. It was a very shallow wooden*

View of the Valley floor looking west up the Cimarron,
taken from the point of the mesa just west of the New
Mexico schoolhouse. Old Roberts Ranch at center.
Photo by Fred Brown, 1992, collection of LaVerne Hanners.

*tray the size of a sheet of typing paper. Into this tray,
they poured a liquified jelly. The liquid set into a ge-
latinous surface upon which my mother or Mrs.
Quimby placed a paper. On the paper they had written the day's lesson or math examples. They used a
special purple ink to write those examples. The ink
soaked into the jelly, and then it was possible to press
clean sheets of paper on that surface and lift off copies. Xerox probably would not have been impressed,*

but it was a miraculous time-saver and very useful.

The schools in the Valley almost reached the ideal teaching situation of the student at one end of a log and the teacher at the other end. We had very little, but evidently it was enough. The descendants of Felix and Stella Goodson have logged an impressive number of college degrees. I would like for all the grandchildren who receive their degrees in the future to remember the ruined stone walls of the New Mexico school and the two teachers who taught there: Stella Goodson and Kathryn Quimby.

CHAPTER FOUR

Ed and D. K.

WELL, ONE THING FOLLOWS ANOTHER. Seems like I will never get to the history of Zadia and my own lives, but I am going to write it all, when I live through some more time here, all sixty years of it. All these things of which I am writing are as plain to me as yesterday and I am going to write all these happenings just as they came along. I am just living this all over again.

I can't even remember what happened a week ago, or a month ago or even a year ago, but the happenings beginning about 1890, for thirty years are as clear as what happened today. When this story begins will seem fantastic fifty years from now. At the same time what happened in these past seventy-five years was quite commonplace and would not be hardly thought of by the people of those far off years. I am fortunate to be able to remember in detail the happenings of all those years so long ago. In fifty years our three children in all likelihood will not be here. That is why I said in the beginning that our posterity will read this history with pleasure. At this time we have twenty great grandchildren. They are the ones who will enjoy this story, for I assume life then will be quite different from the time this story started in 1890.

I will get back to the story. As I said I had found my father Duck Lord, as he was called and D. K. Lord were one and the same. As I mentioned I went over and got a job at $35 a month. I was not forgetting good old Tex. We seen each other often, and I was looking after these 1000 steers, living in a wall tent, 8' by 10', at night we played cribbage, made our bed on pine boughs, had a small cookstove, plenty of dry wood, so we were quite comfortable. Mexican pinto beans was our main diet and syrup and dried fruit. He also had a buckboard. Had to haul our water from the same spring Tex and I used. We had a dozen good saddle horses. When father would take off, I lived alone, and water was so far off, we started digging a well near by. Had about ten foot of dirt then rock when we blasted with dynamite. He and an old miner we knew did the hole drilling for dynamite and I let them down and pulled them up with what is known as a windless [*windlass*], a handle on one side that a rope rolled up on. We worked on this off and on for months, blasting rock and pulling it up in a big bucket is real hard work but my father was a real persistent character in many ways.

One day in particular comes to my mind. I had been out to a dance the night before. They used to dance all night when they had to ride so far most of the boys would bring a quart and hide it out somewhere so along toward morning there would be two or three fights. Where ever there was whiskey, there would be fights.

Once in awhile I would come home with a black eye or two myself.

But this particular morning I got home about sun up and the miner didn't show up that day so father and I worked on the well. I let him down to light the fuse on the dynamite and had him about half way out and that slick crank handle slipped out of my hands and went once around and hit me in the head. I fell right over on that handle and as soon as my senses got straightened out I began pulling father out fast. He was dangling about half way up with a big charge of dynamite ready to go off right under him. That blast of rock would have riddled him to shreds. When he came up and scrambled out of the way, he had no more got clear until the charge went off shooting rock 100 feet into the air. He said in his entire life, that was the nearest he ever came to the very end of his life. I just fell over, exhausted. So he hired a well driller to set over that seventy foot hole we had dug. So we had a well and wind mill in another two weeks. I shake yet when I think of that near accident.

Well, I had another birthday, 18. I took care of the steers. Father went down to Kansas City principally to play poker and be handy to liquor. Went in to see Welch Bros. Commission Co. down at the stock yards. They asked him about the steers. He told them he had the best cattleman in all the country looking after them, me. Well, maybe I was not the best but I rode hard everyday, so regardless of age I thought I was pretty good too. Nobody could tell me very much about caring for a herd of cattle. Good old Tex was always ready to help. As the months went by I did not hear from my father.

There was a real drouth on and the steers were losing flesh every day. I knew they were going to market in the fall and they must be in good condition. I knew a fellow over in Colorado who with two others were stealing calves from a big Scottish concern which ran about 30,000 cows over a range about 75 miles square. I guess they thought that there was no harm stealing these calves from foreigners because they were stealing U.S. grass, which they were. He told me it had been raining over in Colorado and he would pasture our steers for 25¢ a head, a month. I asked him if he and his two men would help me round up and move these steers over. It was all agreed. They came over, those three, Tex, myself and two neighbors, got our steers all together in a couple of days of hard riding, then in one day we moved the whole herd over in Colorado. It was only a 10 or 15 mile drive.

It is hard to believe that Ed Lord could write an entire book, most of which is set in the Cimarron Valley, without once mentioning, much less describing, the Black Mesa. This colossal formation forms the north side of the Valley and runs east for sixty miles from Folsom, New Mexico, to just north of Kenton. The mesa is rimmed with a caprock of black lava. There was no easy access to the top in Ed's day, so he must have moved his steers around the point of the mesa, up on what is now the Tucker Ranch. The "Scottish concern" Ed writes about very possibly was the Prairie Cattle Company. This outfit controlled a spread that reached from Trinidad, Colorado, to the

Robbers' Roost, a famous outlaw stronghold in the eighties,
a few miles north of Kenton. Ed was running his steers in
this general area.
Photo by LaVerne Hanners, 1994.

Indian Territory. According to an article in the Boise
City News, *an 1885 brand book lists seventeen brands
operating under the Prairie name (*Boise City News,
Historical Edition, 1968, p. 16). *This time Ed got his
distances correct. It is about fifteen miles from Sloan
Canyon to the north side of the Black Mesa. The
country there is broken with numerous small canyons. If the Prairie Cattle Company ran 30,000 head
of cattle, it is easy to see how the rustlers could make
a living stealing calves. The thieves could come up out
of the canyons onto the vast prairie land of southern*

*Colorado, pick up a few calves, and drive them back to
the security of the canyons. There would also have
been plenty of room for Ed's one thousand steers.*

I had salt put out on the watering places and these
steers were on the mend from the very first day, in that
very good grass. There had been no stock on this grass
all summer. That was certainly a piece of good luck to
find all that fresh grass in one days drive. I lived right
there with this man with all our horses. They were
weaning these stolen calves on oak brush. I helped them
cut brush and we all looked after our steers. These were
the nicest men to me and I liked ever one of them. We
went to all the dances in the country. They were cattle
thieves but it didn't rub off on me.

They had wolves in that country. So I told them about
Tex. He said, "You just lope over there and tell Tex to
come on over", which I did and he was delighted to find
new trapping ground. There was lots of room for all
these men, who were with the man I was pasturing the
cattle with, and their families. They each lived seperate
from the rest of us. There was a state bounty on wolves
in Colorado. Each pair of ears brought Tex $5.00. The
skins sold high too.

*There were no wolves in the Valley when we got
there in 1925, so I thought surely Ed must have been
writing about trapping coyotes. It didn't seem possible
that an entire species could disappear completely
from a locality in the space of twenty years or so. I
asked Fred Tucker, and he assured me that there still*

*were wolves on their ranch when he was a child. He
said that he had never seen one, but he had heard
them howling and had seen their tracks.*

*Fred was born in 1908, so we can assume that
there were still a few wolves in the rugged breaks
north of Black Mesa in 1915 or so. The disappearance
of wolves from the area certainly demonstrates the
power of a generous bounty. Five dollars a head was
incredibly good money at that time, and we can be
sure that no cowboy or cattle rustler or horse thief
failed to kill a wolf if the opportunity offered. Of
course, Tex was not the only trapper in the Valley. Ed
did lose one steer to wolves, but one one-thousandth
seems a small tithe to pay for the privilege of being
neighbors to those magnificent animals.*

So Tex was in his place he liked best. We went on
through the summer and still not a word from my father. One day in late September, he came in to our tent.
I was not there. No horses, no cattle. He said it looked
like no one had been there for months as no one had
been. He went down the river and asked a rancher who
lived there. He told father that I had sold all the steers
and horses and left there months ago. He believed it all.
So after watching his discomfort, for an hour or so the
rancher said, "Well, D. K. lets go up to the house and
have a drink." "By God", he said, "I need one. To be
truthfull I haven't been around Ed too much but I never
thought he would sell me out like this." "Well," the
rancher said, "D. K., I have had enough fun out of this
so now take it easy. All the cattle and horses ain't over

ten miles from here right now so you go up there and you can find out all about it."

So he came up and I told him what happened. "Ed," he said, "Don't you know you are among the biggest bunch of cow thieves in the entire country, and I don't really expect to gather half of these steers. We must get together what is left of them and get them started to the railroad to ship into Kansas City and 170 miles to Liberal, Kansas." *[The Lords drove the herd to Liberal and then shipped to Kansas City.]*

I said, "Ever one of them steers are here. None of these men would steal any cattle from me."

We started rounding them up the next day. They had not ranged far from that good grass. In three days we had them all together, only two short, one had gone back to the other range and wolves had killed one. He was amazed and the steers were fat. He was about the most pleased person I ever saw. So we started the drive. Tex was determined to go along so we made him the cook. The chuck wagon needed horse power to pull it on those prairies when it rained.

The first night we got about opposite the old range from where we had the steers in the first place. It was raining. Night guard was really a night mare. Everybody was in the saddle, even the cook, but Tex could take it. The cattle wanted to go back on their old range. I wouldn't know what for as they all starved up there in the early drouth, but a herd of cattle has to be trail broke. They did not understand this bedding down business especially in this darn rain storm. It rained all night long and eight of us rode hard all night and to make matters worse, the whole valley was a continous prairie dog town. Two of us had horses step in these holes and both got real hard falls, but these cowboys, it seemed were all hard to kill. A broken leg or arm was splinted up or if they got shot, it seems they all got well quick. They'd get soaked by rain but no one ever got sick. Today, we would all die of pneumonia.

Well, we did not lose any cattle. The next night they all bedded down nice. The first guard of two hours took more riding. The two hours each took two men to each guard. The last guard, one man would just ride behind once the herd headed in the right direction and grazing as they went. He would keep the drags moving up. When his two hours were up the rest of them would have had breakfast and ready to move the herd on. Our Mexican horse wrangler would have the horses up. I nearly forgot him. Horse wranglers seem to be the butt of all the jokes. He also helps the cook. Now, I always thought the horse wrangler really had the hardest job of all. He never got hardly any sleep. He just seemed to sleep when the horses did because he about had to be with them night and day. But these jokes he never could savey anyway. Just about any one of them would fight for this Mexican boy, and nobody must get smart with the cook either. We took this herd of steers the full length of old "no man's land", 150 miles of all prairie and good buffalo grass. The steers fattened all the way. We actually did not drive them, but grazed them all the way and kept the drags from standing still.

There are always some lazy cattle, like lazy people. Just move when they have to. A steer herd is the easiest of all herds to move through long distances. Some of the herds we used to drive up through the Indian Territory were mixed and slow to move because of little calves being born along the way. Sometimes we had to have a calf wagon and they get all rubbed together so their mothers don't know them when we unload at night so as they can suck out their bags. Cows only know their own calves by their smell alone and its a big job to get them mothered up.

Well, the delivery of this herd to the railroad at Liberal, Kansas to ship into Kansas City was done. My brother Fred, met the herd as we got started to the railroad. So now Father, Fred and I were figuring on something. This was early in the year of 1904. I had just turned 19.

CHAPTER FIVE

Back to Kenton

F RED'S IDEA WAS THAT WE BUILD a store in Kenton, Oklahoma, two miles from the New Mexico line and six miles from Colorado, close to the Cimarron River. Father was agreeable to anything, so in that spring we built the stone store building. It was 25x60 plus a large warehouse. I was going to haul in the freight as inside work was not for me. So we got together six good horses and two new wagons. With this good outfit I should do ok.

The photographs that I have managed to gather show the Kenton of the first three decades of this century. The buildings in those photographs look as sturdy as Stonehenge, but for the most part they have vanished. I remember the magnificent stone-work on the Old Beerly garage with the two arched windows and the immense arch over the door. Tom Duncan was the master stonemason of the area. Of course he had helpers, but when we look at the old photos, the remaining buildings, and the old ruins, we realize that Tom Duncan built the town of Kenton.

Ed Lord in front of Lord's Store, ca. 1910. Note the high
dock built for loading wagons, in which one can see deep
grooves cut by the hubs of wagon wheels.
Photo courtesy of James Ford.

There are only four buildings left on the south side
of Main Street. The ice-cream parlor is still there.
Lord's Store, now the Kenton Mercantile, is, of course,
still in operation. In the next block a tiny one-room
building, once used as the post office, stands vacant.
The last building on the south side of the street is the
schoolhouse, now used as a community center.

The north side of the street has fared a little better
than the south, although the ruins there make one

A fabulous view of the south side of Main Street, ca. 1908.
The building on the far left is Lord's Store, the only build-
ing pictured here that still stands. The cars are from the
garage of Lloyd Beerly, Sr., the first car dealer in the area.
The people are all Kenton residents.
Photo courtesy of Lloyd Beerly French.

*doubt that statement. Where Mr. Eddy's Drugs and
Sundries stood, there is an ugly red brick building
that houses an automatic telephone exchange. Next is
the old hotel, the private residence of Joe Bud Layton
and his family. The shattered remains of the old Black
house are next.*

*I talked to some members of the Black family on
Memorial weekend of 1994. They said that the house
had been left completely furnished, but over the years*

Albert Easley, Tom Duncan, and W. M. Eddy in front of
Mr. Eddy's drugstore and post office. Mr. Duncan was the
stone mason whose work can still be seen in the Kenton
Mercantile building (Lord's Store) and in some of the ruins
in the area.
Photo courtesy of Rebecca Walker.

Side view of Lord's Store, ca. 1914. Note hitching rails on
the sides of both buildings.
Photo courtesy of James Ford.

*it had been ransacked and everything in it had been
taken away. The house has mostly fallen in, especially
in the back. Allen Griggs told the Black family hardly
a week went by that someone didn't inquire about
buying the house. They told Allen the place was so
tied up in an estate that the property probably never
could be sold.*

*Next to the Black house are the stone walls that
are all that is left of a building that once housed a
garage and a room on the west used as a dance hall, a
roller-skating rink, and other enterprises.*

*The bank building is across the street to the east, a
solid concrete building now used as a church. Several
homes line the north side. One house has been converted into a Gallery and Gift store. This gallery is
the last house on the north side of Main Street.*

My first freight was oil-cake, a cattle feed made of
cotton seed, shipped up from Texas to Texline, Texas.
Two pounds a day was the regular amount to keep a
cow in good order with good grass. When it rained or
snowed the roads would get muddy, then hauling was a
problem. When freighters got badly stuck in the mud
or crossing sandy river courses, they would have to
uncouple the trail wagon, pull out the heavy lead wagon,
which was a much heavier wagon, then go back and pull
out the trailer. My lead wagon was a 3½ inch, measured
at the inside of the skein. *I asked several older people if
they knew what a skein was, as applied to a wagon. I
also called Sid Housman, who is a musician and singer
and an illustrator of southwestern books, besides being*

Lords in Lord's Store, 1910. Ed, D. K., and Fred Lord are
behind the counter. The young man considering the hat has
been tentatively identified as Tooter Davis.
Photo courtesy of James Ford.

*the only wainwright I know. He couldn't tell me, so I
went to reference books and dictionaries, arriving finally at the* Oxford English Dictionary, *where I found
this entry: "Skein, U.S., a metal head or thimble pro-
tecting the spindle of a wooden axle." In other words, a
hubcap.* I would usually load this wagon with 6500
pounds and the trailer 3500 pounds, making a 5 ton load.
Going in I would always try to get a load in, usually

Interior of Lord's Store, 1910. Front left, D. K. Lord, Fred
Lord, and Ed Lord.
Photo courtesy of James Ford, grandson of Ed Lord.

baled hay or in season, wool from up in Colorado, or
fence posts from New Mexico. I would be about three
days chopping a load of posts. My team never got out
of a walk.

If the reader thinks my freight teams went like the
stage coaches, like in the movies, they don't. So they
never got out of a walk, empty or loaded. I would camp
over night anywhere I might be, pull off to the side of

the road, have a camp fire to cook what I ate, then roll out my bed and go to sleep in it. I had a heavy water proof canvas to roll my bed up in. Many times I have woke up covered with snow. I'd get behind some friendly snow bank to put on my clothes, 15 degrees below zero, with my shirt tail fanning in the cold, cold wind. *Ed was just being modest. He never would have taken off his clothes to sleep in his bedroll. I think he did not want to say it, but he, of course, was removing himself from the immediate vicinity of his camp for an early morning toilet.* On some of these occasions the eight wagon wheels would be frozen to the ground, in which case I would have to raise all eight of them with a screw jack under the outer hub, to loosen them from the ground. The horses did not like those very cold horse collars either, but I had them so well trained that when I whistled they all bucked to the collar that very instant. When six good big horses all started together something had to give. I remember one night in particular. The day had been warm enough to melt the snow and that evening I got loaded up early in Clayton. Every foot of the road was mud. I camped on the Seneca River, ten miles out of Clayton. When the sun went down, it got real cold. All I could do was go to bed. I got cold in bed so by 12 midnight, the ground was frozen hard enough to hold up my wagons. I thought of all the mud I would have to pull through the next day when the sun melted out the roads by noon anyway. So, as I was too cold to sleep, I got up and dressed thinking one thing was in my favor, no wind. I hitched up all the horses and they were ready to move too. That was a bitter cold night. I drove the rest of the night over fro-

Ed Lord (left) and his freight outfit, with Mr. Good
at the reins, ca. 1914.
Photo courtesy of James Ford.

zen roads. I made good time. I walked beside the wagon
to keep warm, as I would have frozen up on the wagon.
I never stopped until the sun came up. By then I had
gotten as far as the Cimarron breaks which is rough
wooded country. I unhitched all the horses and let them
eat hay awhile. I always carried grain and baled hay to
feed my horses. The grain was fed to them in a nose bag
or moral, the Mexican name for a bag to feed grain to
horses in. I built a good fire as there was lots of dry
wood around, had myself a good breakfast, hot coffee
was the main item. I do wish I had the good appetite
now, that I had then. I hauled freight for five years.

Back to the starting point of hauling freight. I was
19 in January of 1904. I never missed any dances if I
could help it. I had met a nice little girl 16 years old,
real beautiful. I soon found I had to have her. I did not

look too bad myself. We both danced well, so we never missed any dances, but we had to go on horses. I thought this was kinda silly, my girl away over there on a horse so one of the guys had a nice buggy, a four wheel hack with a top on it. I was doing ok hauling, so it was not long until Prince was pulling us around in a new buggy with my good looking girl. We were having a real nice time between freight trips. She had other admirers too, but she was my girl all the time, very soon. Anyway, I had the best conveyance. So this little 100 pounds from Texas, I just found I could not do without. She was one of eight children. So, I asked her mother and father if they could do without her. We were going to be married anyway, so every one of them thought I was ok, except the father.

He said, "You don't have any place to live and freighters are a dime a dozen."

He was in favor of a rancher's son up the river, who had a lotta cattle. But anyway, Zadia thought I was ok, so we set a date.

Now, the only preacher was a man who came west for his health. He had T. B. and there is nothing better for T. B. than lots of sunshine and bourbon whiskey. He lived in Kenton. Father was not religious, but he did like this preacher, so ever Sunday he gave him a full quart of Hayners 100 proof whiskey. Believe it or not he had developed a habit of chewing tobacco. Seems like all men chewed tobacco in those days and rolled their own cigarettes. Well this very well liked preacher was going to be the one to perform our ceremony.

So we selected Zadia's mother's birthday, August 14,

Ed's claim shack. This is all that is left of Ed's "mansion,"
and these ruins may not last long, as a deep arroyo is
eroding toward it.
Photo by LaVerne Hanners, 1995.

to have the job done. We were all ready when he came.
He opened his book at the proper place and it began.
When he was bout half through, I seen he was going to
have to spit or drown, so he calmly closed his book and
went to the door and spit out, then came back to finish
the job, and said, "Now lets see, where was I? Oh, well
I can't remember, so I'll start all over again."

I always figured we were married one and a half times, which was better than just being half married. Now we would have to have a place to live as nine people were already living in her parent's home. Zadia said, "We will go live under a tree."

That little saying came true a few months later, believe it or not. We did live under a tree. It will all be explained later. I was now the head of a family. I could file on a claim. One had to be 21 or the head of a family to file on a claim. I remembered the little dug-out Tex and I lived in. It would do to file a claim on, as one has to have a house on the claim filed on. But, I had the freight outfit down at Kenton. I went down after it and came back by and Zadia drove Prince and the buggy, with Mustang tied on the side, and we all went up to Slone Canyon, where the dug-out was.

Our dog was barking inside this hut as the door was open. The pack rats had piled up sticks, cactus and cow dung, to make a nest to have their young in. The cactus was to keep out the snakes that fed on these young rats. I knew there was a snake in there by the way Rover barked. I began throwing out all this nest and getting down toward the bottom. It began to rattle, so I worked carefully as I knew this snake would be coming out soon. Rover knew it too, so as the snake made a dash for the door, Rover had him just behind the head and he soon was a dead snake. He had 10 rattles on him. I believe it was the biggest diamond back mountain rattler I had ever seen. He had already eaten up all the little rats, and old mother rat too, probably.

Well, I cleaned it all out good. Tex had gone back to

Texas several months earlier on a visit, so my idea was to file a claim ¼ mile wide and 1 mile long, 160 acres across the mouth of this big canyon and I could control the whole canyon of about five sections of land. There was live water on it. Then it occurred to me, "Why not file the same size desert claim joining the homestead claim on the end and have another big canyon of five sections?"

The Government allowed these entries, so I needed to go on in after a load of freight anyway, so I dropped Prince and Mustang in a neighbors horse pasture and we both went on in to Clayton after a load. Zadia had two cousins living in Clayton she wanted to visit and a very nice old Aunt. So it took a day and ½ day to load.

Then the next day I filed on the two quarters of land that a near by rancher had been using for many years for nothing. He threw a big fit when he found out I had cut off ten sections of what he called his range. I knew I could beat his ears down if it came to a rough and tumble, but if it came to guns, I knew he was good. He was a middle aged man. At 19 you had to have it, or not have it. I just had to have what was mine, and I made up my mind if I lost I would lose all. I had my gun on me at all times in a holster under my left arm and not visible. It was a Smith & Wesson 38 double action revolver. One button on my shirt was always unbuttoned, so I could get to it easy. I was scared to death. If it was just a fist fight, I knew I was good enough, if it was a gun fight, I was at a disadvantage.

We met, we fought, we both were as bloody as hogs. I had not won this fight yet. But I had not lost it either.

He hadn't went for his gun yet and that gave me a little courage, and he was running out of wind. I kinda felt like he wasn't sluggin as good as he had been. Say, I was getting my man licked. I never felt so good in my life. "Well", he said, "neither one is getting off with this fight." "Oh, yes there is", I said, "I am". That is what settled it. I knew it would have to be done over again some day if I gave in now, so I beat him up good. The fight was over and I was afraid he would shoot me, so I watched him with my hand on my gun. I was scared to death, is why I done my best. I had to win that fight or give up my claims and leave it all. I had as soon died as give up everything. I had a lot of fights on that old Cimarron. Some of 'em I won and some of 'em I lost, but never one like this. It seems so odd, but that man was my best friend for ever afterward. He could have shot me. But I may have got him first. In either case it would have been purely self defense.

I have not been able to find anything about the identity of the man Ed fought. As the man was just using the free grass up Sloan Canyon, his name would not appear on any land deeds or other records.

CHAPTER SIX

Ed and Zadia

W<small>E WERE ESTABLISHED AT LAST.</small> Next thing was getting those two big canyons fenced off to keep the range cattle off of it. I knew once I could show up ten sections of good grass, I could get some backing for cattle. I had plenty of fence posts and freighting was good, so I had the money for barbed wire. I was a fast worker. That is I was used to hard work, so I really did two men's work. Of course I had to keep hauling freight too. My brother-in-law dug all the post holes and helped me build the fence between trips, so things worked out fast. I wanted to build a rock house and get in it before winter, as the roof leaked.

But, I also had a living to make, so we lived in Tex's house until winter. It kept Zadia busy, while I was hauling freight, keeping cattle out of our pasture. The shanty was warm being on the south hill side, but she was always afraid of snakes, and over the mesa south on the Carrizo *[Carrizozo?]* Creek, there lived a Mexican family and one of the men was sorta nuts, going around to the ranches peekin' in the windows. The rest of the fam-

ily said he was only crazy, but that was enough. Zadia
said we would have to do something about it. She wasn't
living there alone any longer.

We moved over to Texline, Texas and had our oil cake
and grain cars shipped to there on account of cheaper
freight rates, and got another freighter for the winter. I
had a large store building to unload the cars into and
we lived in the back. I sold lots of grain and oil cake
from there that winter and loaded our own wagons for
the Kenton store. But, when spring came again, we
wanted to be back on our ranch. Had a house to build
there and we were expecting our baby to come in late
May or June. When spring came we closed up the Texline
store and moved back to the canyon to build on the
house, but temporarily lived in Tex's old shack again.

The very first thing I done in the house building was
to mash a finger with a four pound rock sledge. It wasn't
an eighth of an inch thick and three fourths of an inch
wide, I mashed it that flat. I thought of just cutting it
off with my pocket knife, nothing like that surely could
ever get well. Zadia was there with me so she got it as
round as possible and tore up my handkerchief and tied
it up tight. I went to the shanty and stuck it in a glass of
kerosene, only thing I knew to do. I had four more fin-
gers left, so the rock work had to go on. I think it hurt
less just to keep at work. Small bones kept working out
of that finger for months. When ever I could get hold of
one with my knife, I pulled it out.

It is the tradition of Western people to be stoic.
Pain is simply ignored. My mother, teaching school in

*Española, slipped on a crayon and broke her kneecap.
She continued to teach until the music teacher came
to her classroom. Then she asked him if he would get
the principal to take her to the doctor. "I've hurt my
knee," she said.*

*She raised her somewhat long skirt a bit to show a
knee that was hideously swollen. I went to see her in
the hospital. I leaned over the side of her bed and
said, "You know, Mother, there is such a thing as
being just too damned tough."*

*Mother grinned and said, "You know, LaVerne,
when I remember that my knee was about as big
around as a wastepaper basket, I think maybe you
are right."*

*In the fall of 1993, Fred Tucker decided to climb the
Black Mesa once more. He tried to get his son,
Freddie, to go with him, but Freddie wisely refused,
thinking that Fred at eighty-six probably should not
go mountain climbing. I don't think it occurred to
Freddie that Fred would go alone, but, of course, he
did. He left his house one morning and walked to the
north side of the Black Mesa, a distance of approximately two miles. He climbed the Mesa and was just
about to go the final few steps out on top when his
foot slipped, and he fell and broke his left arm. "I
passed out," he said. "I don't know how long I was
out, but I came to and climbed back down the Mesa
and walked home." It must have been agony for Fred
to make his way single-handed down that steep,
rocky mesa, but he never said a word about the pain.*

Pauly Davis, the son of Tooter Davis and the great-

grandson of Mary Meagher, lived up to the toughness
of his heritage when he made his decision about his
life. He became ill with kidney trouble. He was driving from Texline to Dumas, Texas, for dialysis every
week. He decided finally that he had had enough of
that, so he drove to Clayton to Fred and Reva Rae
Brown's house. He stayed for supper, then Fred insisted Pauly stay the night. They sat up late talking
about old times in the Valley. Reva Rae said they had
such a good time laughing and remembering.

The next day Pauly went out to Kenton to see his
brothers, Bud Henry and Regnier, then came back to
Clayton. He stuck his head through Reva Rae's door
and said, "There wouldn't be any of that chicken and
noodles left, would there?"

At supper that night Pauly talked about his health.
"I know I won't live very long without that dialysis,
but quality of life should count for something,
shouldn't it?" They all laughed and talked and ate
Reva Rae's wonderful homemade noodles, then went
to bed. Pauly collapsed in the bathroom that night
about three o'clock, and Fred barely got him to the
hospital a block away before Pauly died.

Fred still looked stricken when he told me about it.
"I know he said he wouldn't live very long without
dialysis, but I thought he was talking about two or
three years, or maybe five. I didn't know he meant he
would die that night."

"Fred," I said, "Pauly had his two days of quality
life with family and friends, good food, and warmth,
and comfort. That's the way that old cowboy wanted

it, and that's how he planned it all out. I think you should feel complimented."

Except perhaps for Charlie Wire (Girl On A Pony, p. 27), no one ever equaled Ike Like for grim determination when he made his ride out of Miller Canyon seeking help. Ike hadn't felt well that morning, but old cowboy that he was, Ike ignored that until suddenly he began vomiting blood. Ike went to the corral and got his horse, saddled him, and began his ride to his son Chester's place some six miles downriver.

Ike decided to go by the road in hopes that he could flag down a passing motorist and reach help more quickly. Everett, Ike's youngest son, told me just recently about that. Everett said that Ike had to open at least three gates before he got to the road. *"Everett, do you think your dad took the time and effort to shut those gates behind him?"* I asked.

"Why, LaVerne, of course he did. You don't think that old cowman would have left a gate down, do you?"

"I didn't really think so. It's just that it is sometimes possible to open a gate from horseback, but impossible to shut one. I just hated to think about Mr. Like getting down from his horse, opening the gate, leading the horse through, then shutting the gate before he got back on."

"Well, that's what he did all right. Then when Papa got to the road two or three cars went by. Papa waved, the drivers waved back, and went on down the road. I guess they thought Papa was out for a morning ride. Anyway, Papa was barely conscious when he

got to the house. He and his horse were covered with
blood. Chester and I got him into the car and I held
him while Chester drove to the hospital. He was un-
conscious most of the way. The doctor said he was
lucky to be alive and that bleeding ulcers sometimes
were fatal."

"How old was your dad when that happened?" I
asked.

"Ninety-one," Everett said.

We went down to see Mrs. Smylie to tell her I would
be apt to come after her any time now. She said she did
hope some other lady did not have her busy at the same
time. There still was no doctor in the country. But, my
little girl from Texas was equal to anything. Her mother
had a baby boy only a few months back while Zadia
happened to be home, with Mrs. Smylie in attendance.
I wonder why doctors have to take so long to become
doctors. Zadia's own mother never had any sickness in
the family she couldn't take care of. These women from
Texas could do anything. I can't remember when
Gramma Layton ever had a doctor for any of her eight
children. Of course it took two days to get a doctor if
one was ever needed, so one would have got well or
died. No telephones then, of course.

One dark and stormy night it happened. I had Prince
ready and got him hitched up and tied to a tree. It seemed
like a water spout outside. Lightening and thunder, and
it seemed like the whole sky was falling in. Then the
largest bolt of lightening came. Prince just couldn't take
it. He broke loose and he and the buckboard disappered

up the canyon. No use to look for him in that black night. Zadia told me to stay there and get Mrs. Smylie when it was light enough to find Prince. Our baby came. A tiny little girl and believe it or not she was hungry. She came to a good place because Zadia had plenty to feed her. The birth was rough enough for so young a girl. I got Zadia some breakfast as soon as I had the baby taken care of. How could a young girl know just what to do. Of course she had a good lesson when her mother had the little boy baby, but I did just what she told me to do. Now situations like this just don't happen often. I just couldn't believe so young a girl could go through something like this and make it. As soon as I could see, I rushed out looking for Prince to get Mrs. Smylie up there. He wasn't far off and I brought him and the buckboard on in. Zadia felt real miserable. I had to get Mrs. Smylie back as quick as I could. I put Prince in a gallup and it was all I could do to stay in the rig. Mrs. Smylie was in her clothes in ten minutes and buttoned her shoes after she got to the cabin. Prince really made good time. Of course I was bathing him good with a buggy whip all the way. But, I had to hurry. We both just fell out of that rig and got right on in. Zadia was still in a bad way, but so glad to see Mrs. Smylie. Zadia looked like a ghost. I hoped I would never see her look like that again. But she showed spunk just to be alive. But remember, she was from **TEXAS**.

Nearly all the people on the Cimarron River was from Texas. Zadia was in a wagon train of people coming from Texas, mostly from down around San Antonio. There were the Laytons, Zadia's folks, 4 wagons, the Potters, 4

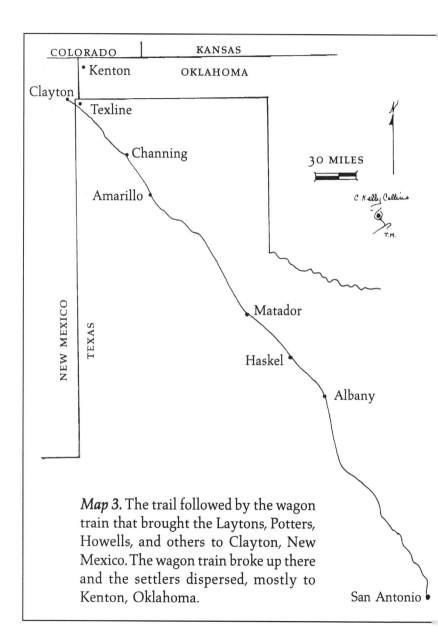

COLORADO | KANSAS

Kenton

OKLAHOMA

Clayton

Texline

Channing

30 MILES

Amarillo

C. Kelly Collins

T.M.

Matador

NEW MEXICO

TEXAS

Haskel

Albany

Map 3. The trail followed by the wagon train that brought the Laytons, Potters, Howells, and others to Clayton, New Mexico. The wagon train broke up there and the settlers dispersed, mostly to Kenton, Oklahoma.

San Antonio

wagons, the Howells, 3 wagons, the Herrons, 2 wagons, and several others. The above 13 wagons were joined by more until there were about 20 wagons in all piloted by Dave Layton, Zadia's father. But, Martha Layton, her mother was the moving spirit of all the women, besides being the doctor. This was in 1895 and Zadia was about 8 years old. It took about six weeks for this train to come from San Antonio, Texas, crossing rivers with quick sand like the Canadian. They had to go as fast as they could or sink in the river. Every wagon had doubled up on teams. Each wagon ordinarily had only one team. They were all happy to be across this Canadian. In that day they were putting Indians in the Indian Territory but at times they would break out of there and come west especially the Commanches. The Texas panhandle, where all these wagons had to pass through was Commanche country and they were warned to keep guards around their horses every night as these Indians would steal them. They came through blizzards up in that Texas panhandle that were really tough. They got over to the Cimarron River valley, all got housing in Clayton and on the river and then the Layton family all took down with the measles. Fine thing to happen the day they arrived.

Right here I want to give a short history of my father's early life. He was born in 1854. His father came from England as a young boy. During the Civil War he owned a woolen mill and made cloth from which the Union army uniforms were made. In the attic of this mill was a pile of woolen waste. A leak in the roof wet this pile of waste, and wet wool will ignite and burn. It developed a fire. He lost the mill and everything in it. He had no insurance. He secured horses and wagons and himself, wife and eight children and moved from Philadelphia to eastern Kansas. He hired out the six boys and collected their wages. He was a regular slave driver. His name, the same as my fathers, David K. Lord. He hired *my* father to a man named Olson, who had a general store in Quenemo, Kansas. It was there he got the experience in a general merchandise store. In 1870 when he was 16, a herd of cattle came up from Texas going to Wyoming. They came that far east to keep away from the Commanches.

Well, father was 16 and they made a good cowboy out of him. But the pay as a cowhand was small and being from a progressive family he was always trying to better himself. He met a man named John Hunton, a squaw man, or Jack as he was always called, who owned a big train of oxen and wagons. They were the large Conastoga type. So, father hired out to him as a common driver, or bullwhacker they were called. There were ten eight yoke teams or 160 cattle or oxen pulling two of these heavy wagons. They hauled enormous loads. I suppose most everyone has seen these yokes that they pull by. Anyway 16 oxen and two wagons were operated by one man. This makes 160 cattle to night herd, and drive up every morning to be yoked up by the bullwhackers. He slept when the cattle did.

It was a hard life, but soon he became one of the bullwhackers and he was so well liked by Jack Hunton, that he was soon wagon boss in charge of the whole outfit. They were hauling Government freight to all the forts around (Laramie, Kearny and Fetterman), who had armies trying to contain the Indians. In the winter time he had them cutting cord wood, the snow being too deep to haul freight.

One of these winter camps was just a few miles from an Indian encampment. While father had gone in to see Jack about some wood hauling to one of the forts, the ten bullwhackers had seen the Indian men ride off on a hunt for game. So they thought it was a good time to go visit the squaws. In fact, they actually caught these squaws and raped them. When the bucks got back they went up to their camp and scalped all ten of them and layed them in a row. What the Indians did to these men is not even printable.

The winter father and I lived in the tent, he told me all about his ten years in Wyoming and Montana. He was in the party who first arrived at the Little Big Horn after the Indian massacre of General Custer and his men in 1876. Many incidents happened to him in that ten years. I have a letter to him from Jack, when my father was foreman of the freight outfit. In it he told him to cut down on his expenses. "Don't feed those bullwhackers canned fruit, get dried fruit, and I see honey on that grocery bill, for Christ sake, honey for a bullwhacker? That's the limit. Feed them beans, potatoes and syrup, and I don't want to see whip marks all over the cattle like I seen the last time I was there. Keep the men busy cording wood up in the hills."

Eventually my father and a man named Smith bought out the entire outfit and paid it out hauling Government freight and supplying cord wood to the different forts over the country. Then they sold the whole outfit and got a cattle ranch up on the Little Box Elder Creek in Wyoming and stocked it. Father came back to Kansas in 1880. He had $10,800.00 in a money belt around him. He took it down to the little bank in Quenema, Kansas and left it there. This was his half of the ranch and cattle he and Smith sold. In 1880 this much money was like a million today. The little bank had a capital of $5,000.00.

Now, he was a man of 26 and with all that money what he needed most was a wife, and the prettiest one in the county. A buggy and a fast team of coal black horses made him the top sucker in all of Osage County. My Grandfather Gibson's second wife had only one child. So she was all fixed up by her mother to snare this rich young man. She already had a sweetheart across the river, but her parents told her she could not see him anymore. It was Dave Lord only who could come and see her. So she was just whipped into this marriage.

Poor guy. He knew all about oxen, horses and men, but nothing at all about girls and women. So, he just got took before he knew what happened. She never loved him. In fact, he disgusted her. All the people in the county were poor. Most of them in that new country lived in shacks, sod houses, etc. Father built a fine two story house on his farm. He was a cattle feeder, always a money maker, so he had everything fixed up in style for his 16 year old wife. He even had Brussel carpeting on the floors. Most floors then were dirt. From the very start it was a cat and dog life for them both.

However along came four children about 1½ years apart, Maude, myself, Fred and Louie. I never knew why any of us were born. Surely none of us were wanted. But, children have a way of getting here, no matter what. I am glad I got here as I have had a wonderful life, nearly 80 now. I could skip the first 15 years with no regret, however, but I had to live the first 15 in order to be here 65 years longer. Poor Maude left us at 19 with her first baby. It died too.

Well, I try to keep this story in order as it happened, but I could think of no better place to put in a short story of my father's life. Poor guy, he had it rough. He was a man's man, but never a ladies man, never! After his divorce out in Kansas, "woman" was a dirty word to him. He was never interested in any more women. He lived to be 69 and was a woman hater until he died. He was a smart man, had a brilliant mind, a hard worker, a very good gambler, as long as he kept away from whiskey. He could about tell if a man had a good poker hand just by his eyes.

Well, I must get back to my own family. Our sweet little girl, Leah, got to us from the day she came to us. We wanted her and we dearly loved her. She got sweeter every day. I don't know which we would have loved the most, a girl or boy. But we loved all four of our children and were glad when they were born. None could be more loved. Not one was ever mistreated. To this day the three living think a lot of Mom and me. They have all given us much pleasure. We were glad to be able to help them anytime they needed us.

Our first baby was killed. I will tell about it now. At this time we were living in Tex's little shanty, already described. During a heavy rain all the dirt I had been putting on the roof to shed the rain got heavier. The breaking point came when I was down in the canyon repairing a washed out fence. I heard Zadia scream. My first thought was that she had been bitten by a rattle snake. When I got to the shanty, I found the whole roof had fallen in. The ridge log had broken in two in the middle. Zadia had pulled herself loose and was out of it. How she ever got out, I'll never know. A cat couldn't have gotten out where she did. Our baby was buried under that ridge log and all that dirt. I started throwing out all that dirt over the wall and out the door, and the poles too. I finally lifted the ends of that log out over the wall and got to our baby. She was smothered, of course. We rushed down to the spring, but could not revive her. The day was warm. I got Prince hooked up to the rig and we went into Kenton with the baby. Bodies cannot be kept in warm weather longer than 24 hours, but Mr. Wilts, an old carpenter made a casket, and the ladies at Kenton lined it and covered it with velvet. It wasn't all alike, but it was all they had. Mr. Wilts had it finished by the next morning. With what whiskey we could find, we kept her sponged off through the night and kept her in fairly good condition. We buried her the next morning. We did not have her but a few months, but she had got into our lives and we can never, never, forget that sweet child, Leah.

Zadia had a badly sprained foot as it got caught in the roof poles some way getting out from under that roof. I came near losing her too, as she could well have been standing near the baby's crib. She was on crutches through the whole ordeal besides her breasts caked, not having the baby to nurse. She was about as miserable as she could get.

We came on back to the canyon the next day and dug our bed out, and also our trunk and a small table. We had no chairs, so we sat on boxes. We were living back under a tree again.

When I read Ed's account of the death of his baby girl, I think of other women whose children are buried in the Kenton cemetery. I think of Edna Gillespie at the grave of her only child, a son, dead of scarlet fever. Above all, I think of Vera Sayre, still mourning her oldest child, Franklin, dead of poison sixty-eight years ago. I talked with Vera about it in January of 1994. She said, "Franklin loved to eat flour, and the sodium fluoride in the box looked just like flour. I had been dusting chickens for mites and set the box down for just a minute. I don't know how much he ate, but we started for Clayton at once. We took him up to Dr. Milligan's office. The doctor said he didn't see anything wrong. I was carrying him back to the car when he convulsed and died."

"Vera," I said, "I was only five when you lost your little boy, but I remember. I remember because of my mother. She had loaded my two brothers and me into the Model T to go to Kenton for groceries. There wasn't a bridge over the Carrizozo then, and you remember the ford was long and sandy. Mother drove right into a sandbank and mired down. Then she looked up and saw the funeral procession coming right behind her. The preacher and the undertaker

had to get out and dig out our car. Mother was horrified and so humiliated that she had held up a funeral procession and intruded upon another woman's grief that she quit driving."

Vera was amazed. "Why, she didn't need to feel like that. I didn't know anything about it. I never knew that at all."

We had the freight wagon to sleep in. More than ever now, it was turning cold nights and winter was just around the corner. I just about worked day and night on the one room rock house I was building. It was 10'x16' with one door and two small windows. We moved the wagons down nearer the house, so I could be working on it continuously. I was building a two room house, also, for a neighbor, as freighting had slacked up. Hauling was seasonal. More hauling in winter on account of feeding oil cake to cattle. I needed money badly, so I was building this other house for $1.00 a day. I got in 12 hours of work each day. He wanted to get into his house before winter set in too. In the winter time, the morter froze up laying up rocks, so I had to finish both houses as soon as I could. We needed the money as both of us needed some winter clothes and we also had to eat and feed the horses grain all the time.

I always had fence posts piled up to haul into Clayton or Texline anytime I got hauling back. I hired the neighbor's team and wagon for $1.00 a day and loaded our own two wagons and the other wagon up and Zadia drove the hired outfit. So we hauled in 500 posts which had a ready sale at 10¢ each and hauled 14,000 pounds

Ruins of the old Wright house, just west of Kenton.
Photo by LaVerne Hanners, 1994.

back to Kenton. Brought home the lumber and corrugated tin for the roof on our house. I was going to be ahead of our neighbors some because in this house we were going to have a board floor instead of bare ground.

Say, when it hailed on that tin roof, it sounded like an army beating on a bunch of tin dish pans. I had to hire a Mexican to help on the neighbor's house so I could finish mine. We got moved in and in less than a week, we had a two foot snow. Say, did we feel lucky to be living in a house. It was only one room, but it was a mansion to us.

While we were building it I had an Indian teepee that we lived in. It was 7' across the bottom and a center pole. Just had a flap to go in and out of. We had chickens that roosted in the trees near by and to help our grocery bill out we had gotten a pig to fatten up on the acorns that were going to waste around near by. We finally had to build him a pen as he insisted on staying in our tent when we went away. Our bed was on one side of the center pole and our groceries on the other side. There was no room for the bed stead, so we had our bed on a heavy piece of canvas on the ground.

We went into Kenton one day for some supplies, in the buck board. As the days were shorter in the later fall, it was dark when we got back and was raining, too. We knew the fuel was all wet so we had decided to just go to bed instead of trying to cook supper. In our absence, cattle had gotten into our pasture and as cattle do, they rub on anything handy, so they had rubbed on our pig pen and knocked it all down and let the hog out. He must have spent the day in our tent as he had eaten up everything and what he did not eat he rooted over into our bed. Anyhow, when we drove up the first thing we saw was his head sticking out through the flap to greet us. I knew exactly how things were inside that tent. But he was just a hog and a pet at that. How he could get all those groceries over into our blankets and pillows, I will never know. I don't think there was a spot as big as a dollar that did not have flour, meal, sugar and nearly a full gallon of syrup, coffee, beans, breakfast foods, in fact all our groceries on it. All we could do was just get in it. What would you have done? with no neighbors within miles and miles and raining hard? How this sweet girl could take much more of what I had to offer is still a mystery to me, after sixty years. Just hard luck seemed to be following us along. How many girls of today would live with a man like me? It would have helped if she could have looked ahead and seen the beautiful life in store for us both. But, I began to think we were both born to have trouble and nothing else. Well, we took it all and just hoped we would get a break some way, some time.

It was so hard to get money to do anything with. There just was not any. A little break came my way in this manner. When I came in with a big load of freight one day, I met a man who had one of the other two general stores in Kenton. He was a friendly, nice man. He said, "Hello, Ed. Will you come over to my store when you get unloaded?"

I just thought that he had some hauling for me, but he said that he had heard that I had a lot of grass up in Slone [Sloan] Canyon. I told him that I had about ten sections that I controlled and there had been no cattle on it for a year; so there was lots of grass. He told me that he wanted to sell me 100 cows. They were old cows, however, that people had given him to pay their store bills. He had been putting them in his neighbors pasture but he needed the grass for his own cattle. I told him that I didn't have any money to buy them with. He told me I wouldn't have to have any money. He told me I could have the cattle for $20 a head and I could pay him whenever I sold any plus 6% interest. All the banks at that time were getting 12% interest.

I took him up on his offer real quick. He wanted me to come and get them as soon as I could so I told him I would come after them the next day if he and his nephew would help me brand them. He had a branding chute there. So, the next morning Zadia and I got up real early, got Prince and Mustang and rode on a gallup all the way down. I was afraid he would change his mind. But he was there with some men to get them branded. I put "ED" up on the left shoulder. We left them in the corral that night and we stayed in town over night, too. I wanted to get them started early next morning.

The two of us got them to their new home that day before dark. They were not in good shape but they started mending right away on that nice fresh grass and fine water, and so did we, for at last we had a break. Older cows are the best mothers, just so they aren't too old. We got living in our house soon after. Now, we were in business. But, we had no bulls. You need a bull for every 25 cows. Bulls can smell a cow in heat for over a mile, so these cows got lonesome eating that fine fresh grass and any bull that jumped the fence, if he was a real good one, I let him hang around. If he was a scrub, I ran him off and set Rover after him. It was not long until I had too many bulls, but the next year I branded 95 calves whose fathers were pure bred herefords. Every calf looked like his daddy. But, I still hauled freight. Zadia was as good a cow hand as I was. That winter was a bad one. We had lots of grass but heavy snow stayed on so long the grass was covered up. I cut and hauled in tree cactus. Close to the cactus I hauled in dry wood. Every morning Zadia would build a fire and with a hay fork to handle the cactus, burn off all the thorns. The cattle were crazy about this feed, as the pods were full of seed. All she would have to do was to give a big war hoop like an Indian and the cattle would come in off those mesas running over each other to get to this good feed. We came through that hard winter without losing one cow.

Things were sure going good, with us and the nicest thing of all, Zadia was pregnant again. We were real happy about this. She just had to quit riding these bucking horses. Mustang had to buck sometimes, just to get it out of his system. This was the winter of 1905-1906. In June of 1906 a little girl came to live with us. We named her Marie. We had made arrangements to be at Mrs. Smylie's house. We were taking no more chances like last time. Marie was a beautiful baby, like her mother. We hoped she would not have the rough early life her mother had. Zadia rode a horse while she carried Marie for the first six months or more. I don't see how she could even get on a horse. She always came back with, "Well, you know I came from Texas", which seemed to mean a gal from Texas gets the things done that needs doing.

That was her mother all over again. With a mother like her, all the impossible things somehow got done. Her mother always had something to laugh about. There should have been a lot more woman like her. She ran into a tree with her car and died of a heart attack years later.

We went through the summer in fine shape. I had all the freight I could haul. Then came another hard win-

ter. We came through that winter, except it was rough
on freighters. On one of my trips to Clayton I was in a
very deep snow. About halfway to Clayton through this
blizzard was an old deserted ranch house.

People who were blocking up a ranch spread would
have no use for all these old houses when they bought
their land, so all these old deserted houses were not kept
up. Anyway I came to this old three room house. The
rooms were all in a row. The center room had a fire
place in it, dirt roof and a ridge log in the center. Also,
dirt floors. So, I moved in while the blizzard raged on
outside. The Mexicans who had moved away left their
poor old dog, so I invited him in. The old picket corral
was nearby, so I chopped them pickets up for firewood.
I put three of my horses in one room and three in the
other and fed them their grain and hay. The rancher
who had blocked up this ranch had kept the wind mill
and tank in good repair for his cattle, so me and the dog
and all the horses were doing o.k. The blizzard raged
for two more days and there was two feet of snow on
the level. Sheep herders froze to death all over the country.

The third day I hitched up and left. There were no
roads visible, they were all snowed in, and a cold north
wind was blowing. I put the dog in the wagon and took
him along, as he would have starved to death. All rab-
bits, rats or anything a dog could catch were all holed
up. I could see what they called the Rabbit Ears. Two
high mounds or peaks visible for 40 miles in every direction. They were north west of Clayton about ten
miles. That was all I could see so I drove the teams all

day through deep snow. Along toward night there was a sort of fog 30 or 40 feet up, but I could not tell where I was going. A man named Eklund had a fence that ran out north east of Clayton and I knew when I ran into that I could follow it on into Clayton. I could not see it but ever few hundred yards I would wade out and find it. There was a settler's old dugout about a mile from town and I was hoping my lead team would not fall into it, but as usual, bad luck was with me. They did fall into it and were so dead tired I could hardly get them on their feet again. I unhitched them and led them one at a time out the door way where there had been steps made. I had unhitched the other four horses so I could hook onto the trail wagon and pull them both back, so I would have clear travel ahead again. All this doing in that deep snow and after night besides. It was far below zero. Well, as I said it was only one more mile to go on in to the livery barn and bunk house in Clayton. The horses, me and the dog hadn't eaten anything since breakfast and we were all ready to fall over. When I got hitched from the wagons, both my ears were frozen, but I got my horses watered and fed first before I took care of myself. I could very easily have frozen to death, but I guess the good old Man upstairs thought I was too tough to die yet. I probably would have went below, anyway.

As I said this winter of 1906–1907 was a tough one. I knew the cattle up in Slone Canyon were in good hands as the country was rough and the snow would soon melt on the south side of all the mesas, so they would have grass and Zadia was there to feed them cactus. I don't know how the cows would have made it but for my little cowboy. I was sure a lucky man to get her.

I became a man January 21, because I was 21 that day. I could vote. But, this is a joke because I done all any man could do at 16, and it seemed to me that Zadia was a woman ever since I knew her. At least she had the capacity of a woman. I doubt if she could remember herself as a young girl. I can not remember or can she, of ever being in a position where either of us could not work our way out of any situation we may be in. If anybody else could do it, either of us could.

Well, the long cold winter was coming to an end at last, but the worse thing that ever happened to us except losing our baby, is what I am going to tell you now. We went flat broke, and worse than that, we still owed $2000 for the 100 cows we bought. Nobody can remember of this ever happening before. I was on the road hauling a big load of freight, 10,000 pounds with six good horses, when I met a man who told me that all the cattle in the country where there was any oak brush for them to eat, were dying. This big freeze came May 1, 1907. Well, our ranch was covered with oak brush, in fact, oak brush was what they eat every spring before grass even started. But, this spring they got a fine crop of early oak leaves just starting to bud out good. That night there came a hard freeze and every cow that ate it died. They could pass no water. There were so many turkey buzzards in the sky who came to eat all that rotting flesh, you could hardly see the sun.

All we could get were the hides. I would slit up all the legs and around and up their necks and drive a 3'

miner's drill in the ground at their heads, leaving the
ears on the hides to pull on, and take a chain to put
around their necks to the drill to hold them while a team
of horses pulled the skins off. We worked night and day.
Zadia could handle a team as well as I. We hardly had
time to eat. It had to be done quick, because the carcas
would rot fast in warm weather. But, we skinned them
until the smell from the rotting flesh would make us
vomit. We did not take time out to cry about all these
nice hereford cattle dying. Being broke was hard to take
and we were having such a nice start.

It was hard to take all we made by hauling to pay off
what we owed on the cattle. The man we owed, John
Tanner, was his name, told us if we never paid it back it
was o.k. What a man. We shall never forget him. I never
thought one minute of not paying him every dollar of
it. It took ten years to do it, but we got it done. He never
asked me to sign any note or anything else when he
turned the 100 cows over to us. We got all the hides
sold at about $2.50 each.

We needed money badly, as I lost a freight horse by
lightning, and just had to replace him. When the first
news came that we were going to have a telephone line
up and down the river, there was already one built from
Clayton to Kenton, I was after that contract to furnish
the poles. The man who sold me the cows was at the
meeting. He told them their best bet was to get Ed Lord
to furnish the poles as he is very dependable. So, I put
in a bid and got the contract at 80¢ each. They were to
be at least big enough to square 4" at the top and in
piles where their wagons could get to them to haul them

to the lines. I knew where all these straight red cedars grew. I did not have time to chop all these trees down and trim them into 16' poles so I had to hire a couple of Mexicans and I worked with them all the time so they wouldn't sit down and smoke cigarets so much. I was paying them $1.00 a day, sun to sun and fed them. They had their own bed rolls. *Sometimes Ed Lord was not very politically correct. He made a few disparaging comments about Mexicans and Indians, but actually not many, considering the times. I have not attempted to sanitize Ed's remarks, because those remarks are also part of history.* Zadia cooked their food, beans, coffee and rice, with raisins in them. The beans had salt bacon and plenty of chili in them. Also, I hired a freighter, as I did not want to lose my hauling while I had the contract cutting these poles. We had to move to different localities for these poles, usually in heads of the numerous canyons, and we had to drag them usually about ¼ mile to where wagons could get to them.

We went up into Colorado to get some of them. We used Prince and the buck board to haul the food, our roll of bedding, also the men's bed rolls, the axes and a small grind stone, as a dull ax and a lazy Mexican sure don't get many trees down. I cleared over $1000 on the telephone pole contract and gave it all to the man I owed.

Zadia said she was sick and tired of this ranch here. She was having too many night mares of roofs falling in on her. She'd wake up in the middle of the night screaming like a panther. With this cattle loss, I was sick of it too. Some deer hunters were up in the canyons and one of them had some cattle back in Kansas he could sell for $2000. He wanted to own this little ranch. I told him I would relinquish these claims to him for $5000. I sold out to him. He was to pay $1000 a year on the other $3000, but he was a real smart young man. He paid off in two years, by buying cattle for the Welch Bros. in Kansas City. He was reccommended to them by my father who wanted Zadia and I in the store with him and Fred. I paid him and Fred $5000 down using the $3000 mortgage and note on the deal, on a one-third interest in the business, and we moved to Kenton.

CHAPTER SEVEN

Moving On

PEOPLE WERE COMING IN and filing claims out in the north prairies and I suggested we put in a lumber yard, and we had freighters hauling in lumber in a couple of weeks. We ordered five carloads as a starter from the Trinity River Lumber Co., way down in Texas. They unloaded in Texline, Texas. We also ordered a carload of red cedar shingles from Oregon. That was a good deal. We had a good lumber yard going very soon, and it was a good business in itself. The store trade grew. It got bigger all the time. One of the two stores closed up and the old store man died. His name was F. B. Drew. Fairchild Barnum Drew. He was a nephew of P. T. Barnum, the old show man. The other store burned down, so this gave us a tremendous lot of customers. Father and I bought Fred out as he and his wife wanted to go to Denver to live. Fred bought and sold cattle at the stock yards and was very successful at it. Then we hired Joe W. Hadden, Sr.

Father started wintering in California. I bought him out about the close of the first world war. Our son, D. K., came in 1908. Were we glad to see him! Our first and only son. Especially since he was red headed. Zadia was the only one of eight children that was not red headed in the Layton family. In 1910, here came another red head, Winona, a cute little girl, especially when she began to have freckles. She had blue eyes like Marie. Dake had brown eyes. These two red heads gave us plenty to do. Dake was bound to stay in the store with us. I don't know if it was because that's where the candy was or just because he liked to be with us. Anyway, we just gave up and let him go where he was the happiest. He never cared for the ranch and the cattle. Winona, when she got older was always on a horse someplace. The wilder the better, like her Ma. If they couldn't buck any they would get one that would. Marie was always the one to look after these two red heads.

Our store and lumber yard kept five of us busy. Kenton occupied forty acres. The east-west road was the main street. It ran past our store front. It was called Lord Street. Father passed away in 1923.

> *Persons who grew up in the Valley of the Dry Cimarron were, like the landscape, passing strange. The people of the Valley were so isolated that the patterns of behavior practiced in the rest of the world did not impinge upon their lives. They developed unique ways of coping with problems and would have been astonished to be told that not everyone would have thought of that particular solution.*
>
> *Brownie Collins met a grievous problem head on. A resident of Kenton died one very hot August. There*

was no undertaker in Kenton and, of course, no em-
balming. By the time the family could get the funeral
arranged, the body had begun to mortify. Despite the
bad odor that began to permeate the church, the family was grimly determined to observe the customs.
The coffin was opened, and the preacher embarked on
an hour-long sermon. Suddenly, the door to the
church opened and in stalked Brownie Collins, carrying a long handled frying pan full of burning rags.
She marched up the north aisle, waving the frying
pan back and forth. She paused at the coffin and
made two or three passes over the body, then continued down the south aisle and on out the door. The
preacher, they say, never missed a beat.

My oldest daughter, Sandy, told me of another
incident at the Kenton Methodist Church. She was
sitting with the other choir members in the little
space behind the preacher, so had a fine view. The
congregation was standing and singing, Alice
Cowart's piercing soprano rising above the other
voices. A bat swooped through an open window and
made straight for Mrs. Cowart. The bat darted under
Mrs. Cowart's hat, grabbed the ear piece of her
glasses in its tiny claws, and hung there head down
while Mrs. Cowart and the congregation sang stoutly
on. When the song was over, Mrs. Cowart sat down
and removed her glasses and the bat. Someone then
kindly took the bat outside and released it.

My own mother was not a little eccentric, although
she would have sworn that she behaved just like everyone else. I was a nervous, high-strung child, easily

traumatized and given to fits of screaming.

It was very cold that winter, and mother had had surgery. Her doctor told her she must keep warmly clad. "Wear long underwear," was his brusk command. Mother sat down with the Sears catalog and ordered three pairs of drop-seated, long-handled knit undergarments. She was dressing by the stove in the bedroom. She had pulled the underwear onto both legs, when she suddenly thrust out one leg and peered down at a small lump that was wriggling and twisting under the cloth. Mother reached down and pushed a mouse out of the leg of her long-handles. The mouse ran across the room into a Post Toastie box we children had been playing with. Mother gathered up the top part of her underwear and ran across the room, lifted up in a soaring leap, and landed on the box with both bare feet. I screamed and screamed.

The women of the Valley may have had their strange little ways, but they were also a gallant and courageous lot. Ed writes a great deal about his hardships as a freighter, and he does give Zadia much credit for staying alone in a one-room house during a terrible winter, burning cactus for the cattle with a pitchfork. She was also trying to take care of a baby. Zadia had to carry water from the well. She had to bring in wood for the fire, and she had to worry about her husband out in sub-zero weather.

Times were hardly less primitive when we came in 1925. We had an outdoor toilet and carried in water from the well and wood from the woodpile. In 1925, however, we had other people around us. There were

men to do the heavy work, and there was swift transportation. Compared to a horse, a Model T provided
blazing speed.

Another woman of great courage was Ruby
Wright. The Wrights·lived up Sloan Canyon. Roy
Wright was seriously ill with nephritis all the time I
knew him, and the family was desperately poor. The
family was also quite large, consisting of five boys
and five girls. Jim Wright, who now lives in Canyon,
Texas, lent me the book on Union County and provided me with various other bits of information. He
told me that his teacher, Kathryn Quimby, saved the
lives of that entire family. When the Goodson schoolhouse opened late in 1936, Mrs. Quimby got Jim a job
with the National Youth Administration cleaning the
ashes from the coal-burning furnace. Every noon Jim
went to the basement and shoveled out the furnace,
and every month the government sent a check for six
dollars. Kathleen Wright was given the job of librar-
ian for the school. For this, she was paid sixteen dollars a month. The twenty-two dollars fed the family
and even bought a few clothes—mostly shoes, I imagine.

Mr. Wright died that year. The next year Kathleen
had to go away for her senior year of high school.
Mrs. Wright moved out of the canyon to a little house
a mile or so west of Kenton. They rented a little two-
room house from Ed Lord for five dollars a month.
Two of the girls, Evelyn and Jane, had married and
moved away, and the oldest son, Frank, was working
away from home. Mrs. Wright took in an orphaned

boy, Denver Webb, her daughter Evelyn's brother-in-law. This made nine people to crowd into those two rooms, but Ruby Wright bedded them down on pallets. She kept them clean and fed and sent them off to walk to school every day. I pass by that little ruin of a house every time I go to the Valley, and I always think of that family. Mostly, I remember the extraordinary courage of the mother, but I also remember the unearthly beauty of all those children. The girls were simply the most beautiful women I ever saw, and all the boys were handsome.

I think Ed was getting tired by the time he got to the last part of his book. He raced through thirty years in two or three paragraphs and, as always, we wish we had more details. We would like to know more about the "tremendous lot of customers" Ed and Zadia had in the store. We would be glad for any detail at all about the settlers "coming in and filing claims out in the north prairies." The settlers did come, and in the first three decades of the twentieth century Kenton and the Cimarron Valley flourished.

The last time I went to Boise City, I saw two great-granddaughters of Albert Easley, Rebecca Walker and Georgia Maxwell. They went into their mother's trunks and brought out photographs of old settlers, neighbors, businessmen, and buildings in Kenton. Many of the photographs had belonged to Ruby Easley, and in her careful way she had made notations on the backs of the pictures, identifying the persons and giving dates. I have tried to recreate the town of Kenton of seventy or eighty years ago and to

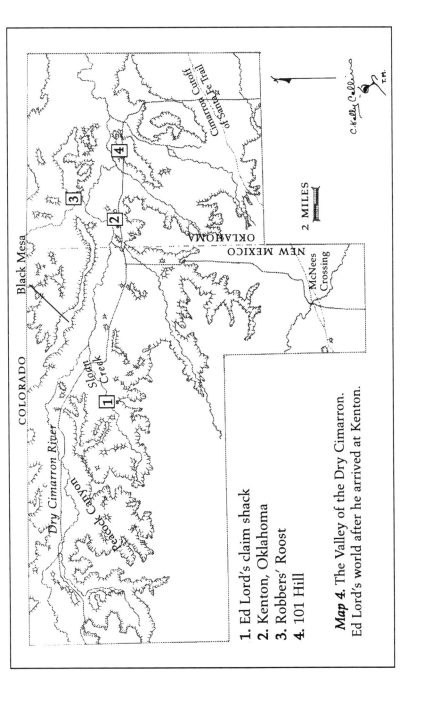

Map 4. The Valley of the Dry Cimarron.
Ed Lord's world after he arrived at Kenton.

1. Ed Lord's claim shack
2. Kenton, Oklahoma
3. Robbers' Roost
4. 101 Hill

View of the main street of Kenton, looking west. Parallel
parking had not caught on in 1910.
Photo courtesy of James Ford.

Henry Beerly and his new Reo in 1909. Mr. Beerly
acquired the automobiles for his garage by riding a
horse to Wichita, Kansas, selling the horse, and driving
the car back to Kenton.
Photo courtesy of Lloyd Beerly French.

*repopulate the empty Valley as best I could. With
these picures that follow and those that I have scattered throughout the book, I seek to present a picture
of the Cimarron Valley and Kenton as I saw these
places when we came down from Colorado seventy
years ago. I have also included modern photographs
that show the continuity of life and customs in this
isolated area of Oklahoma.*

From then on *[1923]* I started blocking up the twenty
section ranch. It joined Kenton on three sides and the
highway on the north side. There were twelve families
on this ranch. I bought them all out in order to get it all
in one block. I was patient with all of them. Each one
came to me to sell out. I never approached one of them
to buy him out. It took eight years to do it, but that was
my plan. They had to want to sell. Then, I would buy it.
Every one came to California to live and they were all
happy there. I never believed in pressuring anyone to
do anything. I carried mortgages on all these places.
They paid when they wanted to. I never asked one of
them for any past due payments. They all were our
friends and those still living are still so. One man's note,
I still have for $500. But, he died long ago and was bur-
ied in the Kenton cemetery, on the land that I gave to
the cemetery long, long, ago. He was a good man, just
unlucky. If I live long enough I want to put up a tomb
stone for him. All six of his children have forgot he and
his nice wife ever lived.

So far I have only got to 1923. There were some
things I forgot to set down. One promise I made to Zadia

Two old cowboys, Bill and Miller Easley, standing in the
doorway of the ruins of their old ranch home, ca. 1925.
Photo courtesy of Rebecca Walker.

Buddy Boy Layton,
cousin to Zadia Lord.
This old cowboy still
lives on his ranch up
close to Travesser.
*Photo by LaVerne
Hanners, 1994.*

Bud Henry Davis, standing in the doorway of the Kenton Mercantile. One of the few older cowboys left.
Photo by LaVerne Hanners, 1992.

when she cried and cried when most all the cattle got poisoned on frozen oak bud. I said that some day we would have a thousand nice hereford cattle and we did in 1932, and on a twenty section ranch. And we owed no one a dollar. There were three other smaller ranches that were ours too. Three sections, four sections, and four and a half sections.

The store we sold to Joe W. Hadden, and his brother Robert in 1938. We sold our ranch and cattle to our son-in-law and daughter, Earl and Winona, in 1945. We have been living in California since then.

Jack Hamilton, son of Andy Hamilton, who lived
up Travesser Canyon. Jack died in his eighties in
1993—another old cowboy gone.
Photo by LaVerne Hanners, 1993.

We have traveled all over Europe, spent a month in
Hawaii, been all over Mexico twice and in every state
in the union several times, so we have had lots of fun in
our later years to make up for those first rough years of
our lives.

But, we would just love to live it all over again. We
love this old world, and everybody in it. We don't know
of anyone who dislikes us. The ones I had trouble with

Bill Easley, Miller Easley, Crompton Tate, and Bill
Clements, ca. 1930. Note white shirts on the Easley
brothers. Crompton Tate was the unofficial historian of
Kenton. Bill Clements owned Kenton's ice-cream parlor.
Photo courtesy of Rebecca Walker.

are all dead, I am sorry to say. On January 21, 1965, I
will be 80. Now that's a lot of years in anybodys language. Zadia is 77, August 27, 1964. She doesn't seem
old to me. She is the best lookin' girl I know.

Here in Leisure World we have to be doing something all the time. Just got a new Buick, so we go a lot.
Have to quit this scribbling just now, and go play some

Old cowboys of Kenton: front row, Henry Labrier, Mart
Eddy, Chet Malm, Mr. Drew, Mr. Gillispie, Albert Easley,
Mr. Ed Eddleman, Henry Jones; back row, Arthur
Brookhart, John Tharp, Cale Giles. This is an unusual photo
because it has Fairchild Barnum Drew in it. Mr. Drew
founded the town of Kenton. He filed on a quarter-section
in 1892 and then became postmaster, and also ran a general
store. His original holding was gradually sold to different
people for homes and businesses.
Photo courtesy of Opal Kohler.

pool. I hope you who are now reading this history, en-
joyed it as much as I did writing it. Some dates may be
a little out of order, but not much.

We eat out most of the time. About all we need more
of is appetite, as we are both sorta skinny. Our doctor
says that's fine, just stay that way. He said the most
important muscles we have are in our arms and should
be used to push ourselves back from the table with. Our
good doctor, E. N. Freeman, up in Whittier, where we
lived for twelve years, kept both of us in fine shape.
There is just one thing more I have to say. It sounds a
little fishy, but it is the truth.

When we sold the ranch back on the Cimarron, we
reserved ½ of all the oil gas or mineral rights on it. When
the uranium search was at it's highest pitch, I bought a
scintilator, an instrument a little larger than a cigar box.
It's on the order of a geiger counter but much more
sensitive in locating uranium. So, we went back there
to search over all this ranch that was deeded land we
sold. Most of the acreage in the ranch is state grass lease
in which we have no mineral rights. We carried this instrument over all this land, staying in a ranch house
that joined the old ranch. We always went up the same
canyon crossing a small but deep wash on the way. Coming back I would lift Zadia up to where she could climb
on out.

This one time out I had some difficult country to go
over so Zadia did not go. I had to jump up about a foot
to get a toe hold, as I did so, there was a big rattle snake
square in front of me all coiled up ready to strike. He
struck me on my nose. I have a long narrow nose, but

he hit it squarely between his two fangs. These fangs were about three-quarters of an inch apart. If this large of a snake had hit me with both fangs, I would have been dead in fifteen minutes, as there was no way to cut off blood circulation, like on a leg or arm. Had Zadia been along this trip, she surely would have been bitten.

I killed the snake with rocks and took him by the tail down to the house, where Zadia was. She looked at my nose. I could not help but think I surely would have been scratched a little by one or both fangs, but nothing showed up. So, there I dodged lightning. I could smell that snake when he struck me. So, that good old Man up there was still watching out for me as he surely must have been for the last eighty wonderful, wonderful years.

ED LORD
Leisure World
Seal Beach, California

POST SCRIP FROM LETTER DATED JUNE 1964

That gal is mad at me today because I don't take off my shoes when I come in. That new carpet is gonna start a war here yet. But it is very nice, different from our first dirt floor in the story. There I could take a chew, and spit anywhere. I don't think you ever knew anyone who chewed. Some people who chewed tobacco could spit on a fly 15 feet away. I knew a woman once who could spit clear across the room (dipped snuff) and hit

the fireplace dead center, and it would sizzle on that log
in the fireplace. I gotta quit this foolin' and wash off the
patio. This damn patio gives me a pain—

E.

*Ed Lord went through all the changes from the
semi-savagery of the cowboy who bathed only once
or twice a year to the sophistication of a world traveler. His changes, of course, parallel the changes in
the country and in the customs of the people. Ed saw
the end of the frontier and the beginning of the space
age. He watched as the cattle industry changed from
the long cattle drives through heat and storms to
huge trucks that thunder down paved roads and over
bridges that span the quicksands he writes about with
such feeling.*

*Zadia, too, went through monumental changes
from a dirt floor in a half-dugout claim shack to a
carpet on which one must not step with a shod foot,
and from having all of Sloan Canyon for a front yard
to a patio that must be washed down every day.*

Ed Lord on horseback.

APPENDIX I

Prologue

The Lords

MY GRANDFATHER, D. K. LORD was born in Lancashire, England in 1828 and died in 1895. He came to the United States in 1841 with his parents. His father also bore the name D. K. Lord.

They had three children, William, Sarah and D. K., my father. His mother died when he was born, in 1854.

D. K. Lord, Sr. was the manager of the Beachwood Woolen Mill, in Cincinnati, Ohio. He bought out the owner and at one time made the blue woolen cloth for the Union Army in the Civil War. It caught fire and as he did not believe in carrying insurance he lost everything he owned.

He remarried a woman by the name of Hanna Simpson and to this second marriage was born seven children. They were all very nice clean, religious children, as their mother was a highly dedicated woman.

After the big fire, he moved his family to N. E. Kansas. About this time he went back to England to see if he could collect his share of a large estate, left by his father. It had been so long the estate had gone into chancery, meaning the government had taken it over. He was unable to get any of it.

Some of the Lords had become famous and some of them had become infamous. They were pirates on the high seas and lost their heads under the guillotine.

Of my mother's family, there isn't anything of importance that ever happened to any of them. They were all nice well organized people, but yet, just people. This is all I know about my folks and now I will continue the story of the Lords with my childhood and life to date.

ED LORD

APPENDIX II

Epilogue

MARIE LORD CORICH WAS BORN June 3, 1906 in Union County, New Mexico. She attended primary school in Kenton, Oklahoma, high school in Kansas, and California and graduated from high school in Clayton, New Mexico.

Albert S. Corich was born in Trinidad, Colorado on April 21, 1904. He attended Colorado University and went into business with his father and brother in Clayton, New Mexico. He is now employed at North American Aircraft in Anaheim, California.

Marie and Bert were married February 7, 1927. They were blessed with five children. John Edward, Albert S., Jr., Charles Ronald, Jean Ellen, and Zadia Marie.

John Ed was born November 24, 1927 in Clayton, New Mexico. He graduated from Clayton High School and Colorado University. He also served 1½ years in the U. S. Army. He married Bertha Ann Lockett in Albuquerque, July, 1953. They have three children, Steve born February 1954, Mark, November, 1956, Lynn, May, 1961. John Ed is Cashier of the Rochester, New York

Branch of the Equitable Life Assurance Society.

Bert, Jr. was born December 25, 1928 in Clayton, New Mexico. He graduated from Clayton High School and married Jo Ann Jacobs in Raton, New Mexico on March 17, 1950. Bert served 3 years in the Marine Corps. They have two children, Albert S., III, born November, 1954, and Sandra, February 1957. Bertie is the manager of the B. F. Goodrich Store in Dalhart, Texas.

Ronnie was born June 13, 1934, in Clayton, New Mexico where he attended school. He was married to Sara Ann Young in Dalhart, Texas. They had four children, Tommy, born August, 1951, Sue, June 1954, Roni Gay, May, 1957, Dee Ann, April 1959. Ronnie was divorced and married Rita Chowning August 14, 1963. His new daughter Debbie is nine years old and was born October 1954. Ronnie is a salesman at the Torrance Furniture Store and lives in Anaheim.

Jeannie was born March 6, 1937 in Clayton, New Mexico, where she attended grade school. She went to high school in Albuquerque and graduated from Whittier High School in Whittier, California. She received a scholarship to Whittier College but decided to forego college and married Andy Meier, Jr. on May 14, 1955. They have five children, in addition to Ronnie's son, Tom, who makes his home with them. Mike, born March 1956, twins Kitty and Chris, February 1958, Kelly, March 1959 and Andy III, February 1962. Andy is a General Contractor and they live in San Pedro.

Zadia was born December 3, 1940 in Clayton, New Mexico. She attended high school in Dalhart, Texas, and Wilmington, California. She married Keith Dreyer in

Kingman, Arizona, August 18, 1956. They have three children, Deni, born March 1957, David, April, 1958 and Danny, October 1962. Keith is employed at Lever Brothers and they reside in Anaheim, California.

D. K. Lord was born in Union County, New Mexico on July 3, 1908. He attended primary school in Kenton, Oklahoma and graduated from high school in Clayton, New Mexico.

He married Isobel Herzstein in Colorado Springs, Colorado, on September 16, 1927.

Isobel was born in Clayton, New Mexico, November 17, 1909 and went to finishing school in New York. She attended Colorado Women's College.

Dake and Isobel had four children, David K., Dee Ann, Linda and Sharon. They lost David K., Dee Ann and Linda at an early age.

Sharon was born August 19, 1940 in Clayton, New Mexico. She attended primary school in Littleton, Colorado and graduated from high school in Albuquerque, New Mexico. She attended the University of New Mexico, majoring in Commercial Art.

Dake was in the gas and oil business and is now dealing in real estate in Albuquerque where they make their home.

Winona Lord Ford was born August 16, 1910, in Union County, New Mexico. She attended primary school in Kenton, Oklahoma, and graduated from high school in Clayton, New Mexico.

Earl Ford was born October 1, 1900 on the Ford Ranch north of Boise City, Oklahoma. He attended Colorado University and was a rancher at Boise City and Kenton for many years. He was also in the oil and gas business until retiring recently.

Nona and Earl were married in La Junta, Colorado, December 28, 1928. They have one son J. Martin II. They are now living in Prescott, Arizona.

J. Martin was born September 12, 1930 in Clayton, New Mexico. He attended military school in Salina, Kansas and Roswell, New Mexico. He graduated from Oklahoma University. He married Georgie Mew in La Junta, Colorado in September, 1954. They have two children, Bobbie and Lisa. Georgie was a war widow, having a son, Bobbie born June 10, 1952. She and Jay have one daughter, Lisa born August 14, 1956. Jay is an engineer for Pratt and Whitney. They are living in Jupiter, Florida.

6 95
nov.
Italo